Crossing the Line

A History of Sports Cheats, Gamblers and Match Fixing Scandals

David Carlton

Contents

Introduction

Throughout the history of competitive sports, there have been attempts to cheat by various means. Whether the motivation is money, the ruthless pursuit of victory, or threats of harm, many sports have been marred by controversy.

From cycling dopers to cricket match fixers to the football betting syndicates of the Far East, and everything in between, the inability to resist the temptations to cheat, for a variety of reasons have been present.

This book examines a litany of sports cheats and, through research, delves deeply into the facts surrounding some of the most shocking cheating scandals in sports. Furthermore, there is a specific focus on the criminal elements of each scandal and the factors that motivated sports stars to risk reputation and credibility by involving themselves in the darker side of sport.

Although there are a lot of technical terms relating to the different sports and mechanics of cheating, they are kept to a minimum for ease of reading and enjoyment. This introduction intends to set out condensed versions of some of the scandals that rocked the sporting world as a precursor to what readers can expect. All of the concepts and summaries are expanded upon in greater detail in the chapters that follow. The links in the references section take readers to sites with different opinions and insights on the tarnishing of sports by cheats.

Firstly, there is match fixing, which has been associated with cricket since Pakistan's Saleem Malik fell under investigation in the 1990s, but the scandal that illuminated the world of cricket cheating was Hansie-gate. Hansie Cronje, the much loved and respected South African cricket captain, was first exposed for match fixing in 2000. The cricket world was left stunned as they learned of Cronje's association with prominent Indian betting syndicates.

Cronje was tasked with manipulating the results of cricket matches as well as influencing team mates to purposefully underperform. As a result, the syndicates made obscene amounts of money, and Cronje and his teammates were handsomely rewarded. Spot fixing was also practiced, meaning that a specific part of the game was predetermined, for instance, a batsman getting out on purpose for less than 10 runs.

Being the charismatic talisman of South African cricket, Hansie Cronje had power over the younger players. When he was caught, the general feeling amongst the rest of the team could be summed up as, "You don't say no to Hansie." Herschelle Gibbs was one of the youngsters who agreed to an offer made by Cronje. All Gibbs had to do was score less than 20 runs in an international match, but when he walked out to bat, his conscience kicked in, and he ended up scoring 74. It is estimated that Gibbs cost Cronje a payout of $150,000, the price of three Ferraris in South African Rands at the time.

Even though Gibbs didn't follow through, he was given a six-month ban and a fine of $14,873. Other players involved also received bans and fines equivalent to their level of participation. These punishments seemed to have been forgotten by several professional cricketers on South Africa's domestic scene. More than a decade later, Gulam Bodi, a former South African under-19 player, was banned for 20 years and imprisoned for 5 years due to his involvement in local match fixing.

Another form of spot fixing is called "points shaving," which was brought to prominence in college basketball in 1951. The modus operandi saw players purposefully not making shots to keep the final score within a certain range. Just like in cricket, the basketball players were rewarded financially. The scandal was known as the "City College of New York Point Shaving Scandal" and came about due to college basketballers being paid a pittance or nothing at all.

Twenty-seven years later, a career criminal named James Burke was embroiled in a point shaving affair known as "The Boston College Point Shaving Scandal." Burke and his gangster associates partnered with Rick Kuhn, who agreed to influence the scoreline Kuhn was in his senior year and a member of the Boston College Eagles. His task was to influence the spread. For instance, if the bookies set the odds on the Eagles winning by more than 10 points, Kuhn would ensure that the opposite was the case by missing shots on purpose to keep the score difference under 10 points. It goes without saying that Burke and his merry men would bet against the odds and pay Kuhn for his favor.

The racket and Burke's gangster lifestyle caught up with him, and after a lengthy trial, he was handed down a 12-year sentence. Interestingly, he received another 20 years for murdering a fellow inmate, which saw him die while still in prison.

A slightly obscure cheating method is creating games that never take place and selling the data to bookmakers. The bookmakers then offer betting odds in the knowledge that made-up results are a perfect science in so-called "ghost games." Criminal gangs have enjoyed success using these tactics, especially in the Ukraine, where fake tournaments involving low-league clubs have been created. Making money is never in doubt; however, the risk of being caught is always present.

Hustling is most synonymous with pool and involves hustlers purposefully playing badly to give possible competitors the idea that the hustler will be easily beatable. Once the competitor is convinced that he or she will win the game, the hustler will propose a bet. When the game starts, the hustler will play to the best of their ability, beat the opponent, and claim the money. Obviously, the hustle is revealed; however, in basketball games, a hustle can be easier to hide.

Tanking, otherwise known as sandbagging, is the act of purposely losing a game for various reasons. In 2019, the Miami Dolphins were involved in a tanking scandal with a bizarre outcome. Allegations that Stephen Ross, the Dolphins' chairman, had offered head coach Brian Flores a significant amount of money to throw games were found to be false by NFL Commissioner Roger Goodell. However, Ross was not out of the woods yet. He was given a limited suspension and fined a whopping $1.5 million for violating the integrity of the game by trying to secretly convince Tom Brady to make a move to the Dolphins while still under contract with the New England Patriots.

Bruce Beal, the vice chairman of the Miami Dolphins at the time, was in cahoots with Ross. He was accused and found guilty of having discussions with Tom Brady in 2019 and 2020. Beal reported back to Stephen Ross and other Dolphin executives on a regular basis. These communications continued during and after the 2021 season, at which time Brady was contracted to the Tampa Bay Buccaneers. The discussions were about Brady becoming a minority partner and executive at the Dolphins, with the possibility of becoming a player.

In early 2022, prohibited conversations took place with Don Yee, the agent of the New Orleans Saints. Bruce Beal's intention was for the Saints' coach, Sean Payton, to serve as coach of the Miami Dolphins. Stephen Ross was not involved in the discussions directly, but just like in the Tom Brady situation, he was kept informed by Beal. Although these incidents didn't amount to on-field cheating, their severity and audacity shocked football players and supporters on an unprecedented level. Like Stephen Ross, Beal was handed down a limited suspension but was fined $500,000, significantly less than Ross but much more than a slap on the wrist.

The above three sets of sporting scandals were motivated by money, but many other sports cheats have been driven by the desire to win at all costs. Arguably, the most infamous "win at all costs" sportsman was Lance Armstrong. The disgraced former legend popularized cycling immeasurably, as he obliterated the competition in seven consecutive Tour de France races after having beaten testicular cancer.

His success inspired the Lance Armstrong Foundation, a non-profit organization dedicated to raising awareness and funds for cancer patients worldwide. He released an inspirational and goosebump-inducing book, *It's Not About the Bike: My Journey Back to Life,* in 2000. He met with presidents, appeared on talk shows, gave motivational talks, and was loved by millions while hiding the seedy underworld of professional cycling. The sport had long been marred by the use of performance-enhancing drugs; however, the Armstrong scandal uncovered a well-oiled, precision-fueled doping machine like no other.

Interestingly, Armstrong never tested positive in a doping test, but the jury is still out regarding the truth of the claim. In any event, it was not a positive test that outed Armstrong, but rather his teammates, who could no longer in good conscience keep up the ruse. The major individuals in revealing near-constant doping over several years were Frankie Andreiu, prompted by his wife Betsy, as well as Floyd Landis and Tyler Hamilton, amongst others.

Armstrong's teammates were also doping throughout. However, the argument is that Lance intimidated them to the point where they felt that they had no choice but to carry on doping and carry on covering it up. This was no amateur operation and was led by Dr. Michele Ferrari, whose shady reputation was born in 1994 when he made controversial comments about the performance of EPO.

Erythropoietin (EPO) is a hormone produced primarily by the kidneys that stimulates the production of red blood cells (erythrocytes) in the bone marrow. The primary function of EPO is to increase the number of red blood cells in the body, which helps to transport oxygen to the body's tissues. This can improve endurance and physical performance, which is why it has been used as a performance-enhancing drug in sports.

There are several ways to use EPO as a doping agent, but arguably the most common, especially in cycling, is to draw blood, preserve it, and re-inject it. Transfusions can also be used, as well as chemical stimulation to create more red blood cells, having the same effect.

There's a lot more to the story, as there is with match fixing, spot fixing, point shaving, ghost games, and hustler stories, to name a few. But how much of a threat is this improper conduct to the sportsmanship and fairness of competition?

Well, the threats are different in different sports, and cheating to win as opposed to cheating to lose are factors that can't be ignored. In addition, cheating for no purpose also exists, as in the case of influencing a spread but still winning the game.

Fixing a game for a purposeful loss takes away the competition element. If the winning team is unaware that the match was thrown, they will carry the pride of winning without realizing that they may have lost had the other team played to the best of their ability. Most often, match fixing is in pursuit of money, but throwing a match in a tournament in order to face a weaker team in a semi-final combines cheating to lose and cheating to win.

To use cricket as an example, Australia, India, and England are arguably the three best teams in the world. Australia faces India in a pool game; if they win, they will come up against England in the semi-final; if they lose, they will play Zimbabwe. Considering that Zimbabwe is weaker and has only beaten Australia once in three decades, an Australian win is virtually guaranteed. There doesn't appear to be any evidence of this ever happening, so I must stress that it is just an example that clearly illustrates cheating to lose in one game in order to win in the next game.

After a cheating scandal, we often hear the term "bringing the sport into disrepute," which is an apt description of what cheating does. In such cases, sportsmanship goes out the window, and respect is lost by fellow athletes, coaches, and the general public.

The absence of sportsmanship and the grossly unfair conduct of Lance Armstrong is one of the best illustrations. When Armstrong was stripped of his seven Tour de France titles, the second-place finishers were not retrospectively awarded first place. Let's assume for these purposes that the respective second-place finishers were not using banned substances. Armstrong's doping meant that they were robbed of glory, money, and prestige as they fell victim to grossly unfair competition.

Armstrong blew sportsmanship and fair competition out of the water, but it doesn't seem like the popularity of cycling was hugely affected. Of course there were and still are detractors; however, there are no concrete statistics as to whether cycling has a smaller following. If we assume that the sport was cleaned up after the Armstrong scandal, then it follows that competition is fair and that participants in professional cycling display good sportsmanship.

It would probably be accurate to say that after a sports cheating scandal, the athlete is hated, but the sport is not. The public perception may be that the culprit has been banned and the sport has gone back to being fair. However, the public may write off the sport after concluding that even though the culprit has been banned, the sport remains tainted. One may conclude that with time, scandals are forgotten, or at least not thought about, and credibility returns.

Before I get into the body of this book, there is a discussion point that I must mention. The influence of live broadcasts and the internet on modern-day sport, specifically in relation to betting, The former has an impact in terms of the analysis of the game, the athletes, and the odds. Being able to get this information immediately and without leaving home holds a slight advantage over going to the track or the tote, to use an obvious example.

If you are a football (soccer) watcher, you will know that in-studio build-ups to games involve extensive discussion by experts. Analysis and statistics are discussed, as are player form, the history of wins and losses at the venue, and possible tactics to suit weather conditions, among other topics. This allows sports gamblers to be informed and thus theoretically stand a chance to place more accurate bets.

Betting sites go hand in hand with information, and anyone with access to a smart phone can download a betting app and place bets in real time. A good example is golf, where you can bet on certain players to get certain scores on specific holes. The addiction is how immediate the process is. If you understand golf and pay attention to the commentary, it is likely that you will place a well-thought-out bet. During golf tournaments, player statistics will be displayed on screen and can be semi-accurate indicators of a player's score on an upcoming hole. For instance, if a golfer's statistics show that he or she has hit 90% of par-3 greens in one shot over the course of a season, the chances of that golfer doing the same on a par-3 that you want to bet on are high. Let's say, for instance, that the same golfer's statistics show that he or she has a 70% record of two-putting on par threes; the chances of it happening again are pretty good. Based on the statistics, if you bet on the golfer to par the hole (3 shots), you have made an informed choice and stand a greater chance to win.

Chapter 1

Baseball

Referred to as America's national pastime, and with a history spanning back to 1846, baseball has captivated millions of fans across the United States and the world. The sport is played in over 100 countries, and the US MLB has attracted players from Panama to Brazil to Germany and more. Given these statistics, it is no wonder that over the years, cheating scandals have arisen. Let's start with the biggest and most shocking of the scandals.

The Black Sox Scandal

The year was 1919, and the Chicago White Sox faced the Cincinnati Reds in the MLB World Series. Several players were involved in a plan to throw the game, and thereafter, it took seventy-four years for the White Sox to win a World Series, prompting critics and fans alike to believe that the 1919 scandal placed a curse on the men playing out of Chicago, or so the legend goes.

The Scheme

Money was the motivator, as it so often is, and the scheme was first discussed by a gambler named Joseph "Sport" Sullivan and a talented White Sox first baseman, C. Arnold Gandil. Interestingly, Sullivan got the nickname "Sport" for his good looks and charm, not for his sports betting prowess, which is somewhat ironic. The meeting between the gambler and the player saw the former offer the latter a sum of money to tank the game.

Sullivan was no stranger to paying out money to players, but until 1919, the exchange had been for insider tips, instead of throwing the World Series. Sullivan's proposed scheme was outrageous and unprecedented at the time, but by all accounts, his calm and cool demeanor was used effectively to draw players in. Of course, money played a role as well.

Having said that, it did take some convincing to get Gandil on board, but the first baseman could not resist a payout of $100,000. In today's equivalent terms, the amount would be over $1.7 million, and considering that in 1919, players were poorly played, Gandil was unlikely to turn the offer down.

Gandil couldn't do it on his own, so he began recruiting teammates. Shortstop Charles Risberg and outfielder Oscar Felsch were first on the list, and they were accompanied by two pitchers, Eddie Cicotte and Claude Williams. Buck Weaver was initially included, but the third baseman took a moral stance and pulled out. The group of tankers expanded when infielder Fred McMullin had to be added as a result of overheard conversations. The final tanker was pitcher Joe Jackson, who completed the syndicate.

There was speculation that several other individuals were involved, but definitive proof has never been brought forward. A possible reason is that Sullivan, most likely without the knowledge of the syndicate or at least with limited knowledge, brought in two former players, Bill Burns and Bill Maharg. Burns had ended his career at the White Sox, and Maharg at the Detroit Tigers. Sullivan's goal was to raise the money with the help of the aforesaid individuals, with help from mob boss Arnold Rothstein and boxer Abe Attell.

Some baseball fans may argue that the scheme was poorly concealed from the start because the odds, initially heavily in favor of the White Sox, began to shift to the Cincinnati Reds. The reason for the shift was the obscene amounts of money being placed on the Reds in the lead up to the first of nine fixtures. Rumors of gamblers and players conspiring began to spread, as could be expected due to the enormity of the suspected scheme.

Suspicions grew during the first game on the 1st of October, when Eddie Cicotte uncharacteristically hit the Reds batter with the opening pitch. The word was that hitting the batter was done on purpose as a signal to confirm that the tank was on. Cicotte, usually a measured player, had a terrible game, and the absolute thrashing (9–1) indicated that Cicotte and the other White Sox players involved had thrown the game in an exaggerated and obvious manner.

The second game garnered a more realistic scoreline (4–2), but Claude Williams, the five-season White Sox pitcher, all but gave away the ruse by walking three batters in a row. Nobody had come up with concrete proof, but suspicions grew, as the White Sox continued to lose, and were 4–1 down after 5 games. By this point, the conspirators were becoming angry because the gamblers had not paid out as much as they had promised. In retaliation, the players involved made a suspected call to go against the plan and put in every effort to win the World Series.

Recovering from a 4–1 deficit would prove difficult, but the White Sox gave themselves a chance as they clawed back two games, leaving the series score at 4–3. Two more wins, and the White Sox would be World Series champions, but they lost in the eighth game, handing the Reds their first World Series. The score in game eight was 10–5, which was a possible indication that the players had changed their minds again and went back to tanking.

A change of mind was a real possibility when considering that a mob boss and renowned gamblers were involved. As is the case with the mob, threats of harm were allegedly made, which became the determining factor. It is possible that the White Sox were legitimately beaten, but it was of no consequence, as the gamblers won packets of money, as was the goal of the scheme from day one.

Rumors of tanking were still rife, and after a few months, an opinion piece was published in the New York Evening World by Hugh Fullerton, a prominent sports journalist. The article explored the possibility of gamblers and players conspiring to manipulate results. Charles Comiskey, the White Sox owner, hit back immediately, denying any such behavior; however, it came to light at a later stage that Comiskey was tipped off but didn't take any action.

As 1919 turned into 1920, the baseball community fell silent on the unproven tanking theory. However, the wound was scratched open when it came to light in August 1920 that gamblers and players from the Philadelphia Phillies and the Chicago Cubs had been involved in manipulating results. These revelations sparked interest in the White Sox affair, which was blown wide open when Bill Maharg publicly admitted his involvement. Cicontte was the next canary to sing, and within two months, Gandil, Williams, Felsch, McMullin, Weaver, and Jackson had been indicted. The syndicate became known as theBlack Sox" and faced nine charges of conspiracy; however, the court papers were "lost," the confessions became void, and the prosecution team was dead in the water.

In an unprecedented move, Judge K.M. Landis, the first-ever baseball commissioner, issued life bans to the eight players involved and did so with contempt. As just punishment was dished out, it was confirmed that the Black Sox scandal was the biggest and most outrageous scandal in baseball history. It still remains so today, but was it worth it for the shamed players? It is a difficult question to answer, as there is no definitive evidence that they received the money due to them, but the embarrassment and damage to the game more than likely provided sufficient long-term guilt. Unfortunately, future players did not learn from the infamous scandal; perhaps the Black Sox affair was forgotten sooner than it should have been.

The Astro's Cheating Scandal

Fast forward to 2017 and another scandal—very different from the White Sox scandal, but still worthy of news headlines. As the cheating modus operandi unfolded, it got more complicated for the perpetrators, and when the scandal was revealed, the MLB was forced to extensively investigate. To this day, the players have not shaken the title of cheats and probably will not do so for the rest of their lives.

The Scheme

Individuals working for the Houston Astros sat comfortably in the video room during games and paid close attention to the feed from the center field camera. The reason for studying the feed was to pick up on signals made by opposing teams and to communicate such signals to the batter. The scheme was complicated in that the message was relayed to the dugout, then to the second base runner via a subtle signal, and from the second base runner to the batter in an effort to inform that batter what to expect from the upcoming pitch.

The methods of communication between the video room and dugout involved the coach dialing the video room and/or text messages being sent from the video room to a smart phone or watch kept in the dugout. Not a particularly genius move, but one rooted in practicality.

The Astros bench coach during the scandal was a man by the name of Alex Cora, who partnered with several players, the most prominent of whom was Carlos Beltran. He was a hitter for the Astros and improved the scheme by getting Cora to place a monitor that received the live feed on the side of the dugout. Upon viewing the live feed, certain players in the dugout would clap, whistle, or shout toward the batter. Hitting a trash can in a morse code kind of way proved more successful than the other three methods and thus became the preferred communication channel.

Among suspicions that the Astros were sign-stealing, the Boston Red Sox were caught for the same thing in September 2017. This prompted the office of the MLB commissioner, run by Rob Manfred, to send out a stern communication stating that replay equipment must not be used for sign stealing under any circumstances. The communication further stated that team managers and field managers would be held responsible should it come to light that a team is operating against the instructions of the commissioner's office. Included in the communication were carefully framed, mild allegations that the Astros had engaged in sign-stealing throughout the entire 2017 season. It was almost an inference, without full commitment to a full-blown accusation.

Banging on trash cans to communicate came to an end in the 2018 season, but it was believed that the Astros carried on exchanging messages with the video room. It was audacious of the Astros to stretch the scheme for so long, but it was found that from the postseason of 2018 onward, they abandoned the scheme. One would like to believe that the abandonment was conscience-motivated, but all indications are that the methods were no longer effective.

The Culprits

Rob Manfred compiled his official report in 2019, in which he recorded that the offenders included most of the players, Coach Cora, and a handful of low-rung operational employees. Manfred's earlier communication stating that managers would be held responsible for sign-stealing meant that none of the players were punished in any way. During investigations, it came to light that one of the managers, A.J. Hinch did not approve of the scheme and was not a part of it in any capacity. Hinch admitted that he made no attempt to stop the goings-on and never mentioned his disapproval to Cora. Manfred found further that Jeff Luhnow, general manager of the Astros, was made aware of the scheme by way of emails received. Luhnow denied these findings, but the speculative common opinion was that, at the very least, he knew about them but paid little attention.

The Whistleblower

Mike Friers, a former Astros pitcher, sat down with two sports writers, namely Ken Rosenthal and Evan Drellich, in November 2019 to "blow the whistle," as it were. On the 12th of the same month, a joint article by the two sports writers was published in The Athletic, containing the damning truth as told by Frier. By this time, Frier was playing for the Oakland Athletics after a stint with the Detroit Tigers. Opinions were divided as to whether Frier had clawed back his own integrity and the integrity of the game, or whether waiting a while before talking was a disingenuous move.

The Punishment

As part of a team punishment arrived at by Rob Manfred, the Astros forfeited their first and second round picks in the 2020 and 2021 drafts. Any picks thereafter would be lost if compensation for signing a free agent ensued. Manfred also imposed a fine of $5 million, as he took a hard stance, considering that the amount was the highest fine permitted.

Jeff Luhnow was dealt a suspension from January 2020 until the conclusion of the World Series in the same year. He was not allowed to use any of the club's facilities and was not allowed to work for the Astros or any other team. A.J. Hinch was handed the same punishment, and both men were subsequently fired by the Astros. Coach Cora was also suspended in 2020, but he rejoined the Red Sox in early 2021.

The obvious anomaly is that none of the players received any sanctions, in light of Manfred's stern communication discussed above. Perhaps Manfred should have included players in disciplinary measures, but it was too late. He definitely took a hard stance in imposing the maximum fine and dishing out serious suspension-related punishments, and it could be argued that Manfred restored credibility to the game.

The Pete Rose Betting Scandal

When Pete Rose was handed a lifetime ban in 1989 for various betting infractions, one would have thought that he questioned his integrity and felt shame and embarrassment. Considering that Rose launched a gambling podcast in 2021, it would not be remiss to have the opinion that his ban was water off a duck's back, but only Rose can decide on that one.

Rose, known as "Charlie Hustle," had a 23-year career in Major League Baseball, where he secured three World Series victories and won a plethora of awards. To this day, he still holds the all-time MLB hit record, and a good argument can be made that he is one of the greatest players to pick up a bat. After retirement, he managed his former team, the Cincinnati Reds, until his fall from grace in 1989. It took Rose fifteen years to admit his wrongdoing after denying any involvement on countless occasions. He was charismatic, entertaining, and larger than life, but he will never shake the reputation of being one of the biggest gambling cheats in the history of baseball. Rose was basically a gambling addict, and like all addictions, gambling catches up with you.

The Scheme

To some, it can't be called a scheme because it would appear that Rose placed bets on his own team without tanking or influencing any other individuals in sports betting circles. Yes, it was illegal, but on the other hand, he always played to win, or so the public has been led to believe. There are always cynics, and Rose's other personal controversies, including suspicions of statutory rape and proven tax fraud, probably vindicate the cynics, but the waters have always been slightly muddied.

Rumors had been abounding for some time, but on March 20, 1989, Peter Ueberroth announced that the MLB commission would be launching an inquiry into Rose's personal and business affairs. The media had a field day, especially when the news that the federal authorities would also be involved became public. Tales of associations with convicted felons, outrageous betting losses, and the murky handling of Rose's autograph signings and memorabilia auctions came to light. Due to the seriousness and intricacies of Rose's behavior, John Dowd, an experienced and respected Washington, D.C., lawyer, was appointed as special counsel to lead the investigation.

Dowd's report detailed allegations that in 1985, 1986 and 1987, Pete Rose was heavily involved in gambling. Below is a direct quote from Dowd's said report (1989): "Testimony and the documentary evidence gathered in the course of the investigation demonstrated that Pete Rose bet on baseball, and in particular, on games of the Cincinnati Reds Baseball Club, during the 1985, 1986, and 1987 seasons."

Rose's first admission of guilt, as mentioned previously, was made in 2004, when he released his autobiography. Well-known author Rick Hill worked with Rose in putting together the book, entitled "*My Prison Without Bars*." Strangely, Rose had accepted his lifetime ban in 1989, foregoing any chance of being inducted into the MLB Hall of Fame. A lot of questions were raised as the insinuation was that an innocent man would fight his case, but when Rose published his admissions, his guilt had long before been confirmed in the court of public opinion.

The shamed baseball great said that he only bet on the Cincinnati Reds during his years of managing the same team that he played for prior to his retirement. Rose stated that, on occasion, he would place bets five times a week. Maybe he was sensationalizing and thought that if he broke the story, he had better make it as scandalous as possible, with some serious exaggeration. Who knows.

Due to his ban, Rose was not eligible for the MLB Hall of Fame, but he tried his damndest to be placed on the ballot. His final effort to be considered was made in 2016 when he petitioned the Hall of Fame requesting that he be given permission to submit his name for consideration. Rose was unsuccessful, however he was inducted into the Cincinnati Hall of Fame in the same year.

Pete Rose was just one of those individuals who could not stay out of trouble but was still loved by fans. In fact, despite all his unsavory behavior, Rose was given a standing ovation at Pacific Park in San Francisco. The occasion was a promotional event before a World Series game in 2002, and the ovation lasted for more than a minute, along with chatter of "Hall of Fame! Hall of Fame!" from the excitable crowd. Yes, that was before his book, but the success of his podcast is evidence that the man nicknamed "Charlie Hustle" is a baseball legend in the eyes of the public.

The 1994 Cleveland Indians Corked Bat Incident

In the mid-nineteenth century, players made their own bats, with no restrictions on weight, size, or material. However, in 1859, a set of regulations was established that limited bat length and diameter, but around 1884, the now world-famous Louisville Slugger bat was crafted out of wood. Over the years, size, shape, and dimensions changed slightly, but wood remained the primary material. In 1924, a man by the name of William Shroyer secured a patent on the world's first known metal bat. It took almost fifty years for metal bats to gain wide usage, and from the 1970s on, aluminum and, later, titanium bats became the norm, as we see today. However, in the summer of 1994, a surprisingly brazen corked bat swapping incident took place during a division game between the Chicago White Sox and the Cleveland Indians.

The existence of corked bats is no secret; they are used in amateur leagues, social baseball, and on training grounds, but are not permitted in the MLB. There are two reasons, the first being that a corked bat is more likely to shatter and cause injury. The second reason is fair play; cork bats are lighter and increase swing velocity, meaning that the ball travels much further than if hit with an aluminum or titanium bat.

Before the game started, White Sox manager Gene Lamont was informed that one of the Cleveland Indians was going to use a cork bat. The alleged culprit was Albert Belle, and after Lamont reported him to the umpires, his bat was confiscated and locked up in the umpires' change room. That was that, or so Lamont thought, but during the game, a reserve pitcher for the Indians named Jason Grimsley was tasked with what can only be described as a seriously stupid plan!

Grimsley was instructed to crawl into the ceiling, then through to the umpire's room, climb down, retrieve the corked bat, and swap it with a non-corked bat. Dave Phillips, one of the umpires, discovered the scheme when he went into the change room and noticed immediately that there was damage to the ceiling and that residue was lying on the floor. What made things worse for Grimsley is that the replacement bat was branded "Paul Sorrento," which was not the case with the cork bat.

The plan was truly idiotic and resulted in a ten-game ban for Belle, which was reduced to seven. Probably too lenient, but on the scale of baseball scandals, it was regarded as minor.

The Pine Tar Incident

Other than creating a scandal in an MLB fixture in April 2014, the Boston Red Sox pitcher gave the media some good material for silly puns, such as "Tar for the Course." The incident was more comical than anything else, but nonetheless, it was definitely cheating.

The suspicion was that the New York Yankees pitcher, Michael Pineda, had pine tar concealed on his body, which he was not so subtly using to improve his grip. The crowd erupted with cheers as umpire Gerry Davis approached the mound after Boston Red Sox manager John Farrel requested a time-out. At first, the cheers may not have been due to the knowledge of the pine tar but rather to the excitement that something big was about to happen.

Davis patted Pineda down in a humorous search attempt and discovered the tar on Pineda's neck after a few minutes. The pitcher was not so politely kicked out, as the home crowd let out cheers and jeers. He was branded a cheat and handed a suspension of eight to ten games. Joe Giraldi, the Yankees manager, couldn't find many words to explain, so instead he moved a camera that was following Pineda into the tunnel. It was as if Giraldi was trying to pretend that it didn't happen or maybe making an effort to allow Pineda a bit of "privacy." Giraldi's move only added to the funny nature of the whole saga. It was widely believed that pine tar was extensively used in the MLB and that Michael Pineda was the unlucky one to be caught and disciplined. Despite being a laughingstock, Pineda remained a cheat, but he was successful in regaining his credibility as the public "forgot" about the incident over time.

Chapter 2

Basketball

The man who invented basketball was Scottish! Who would have thought? He wasn't born in Scotland, but his parents were Scots who had settled in Canada. James Naismith was his name, and he arrived in America in 1890. Naismith began teaching physical education at the International YMCA Training School in Springfield, Massachusetts, after his arrival in the States. When a severe blizzard littered the town with many feet of snow in the winter of 1891, Naismith's students grew exceedingly restless due to not being able to go outside and burn off their youthful energy.

Naismith got the boys into the gym and tried to arrange a semi-physical game of football, but it didn't resonate with his students, who became increasingly filled with excess energy. Naismith knew the rules of rugby from his Scottish parents and had previously played lacrosse, so he started thinking of ways to combine them in an effort to develop an indoor sport. He drew on an ancient game that he played with his friends and siblings as a young boy called "duck a rock," which involved throwing stones at a large rock placed on a raised surface, usually a tree stump.

The game that would later be called basketball was developed by Naismith on December 21, 1891. His initial idea was to split the boys into two teams and give each a chance to throw a soccer ball into a box in order to score a point. All he could get his hands on were baskets used to carry peaches in the summer. Naismith got the eager students into the YMCA gymnasium and affixed a basket to the balcony on one end of the gym and a second basket on the other end. The height of the baskets was roughly three meters, but only because that was the height of the balcony. Although the game has evolved considerably, the height remains the same. Next, Naismith got nine boys on one side of the gym and nine on the other, threw a small soccer ball in the air, and blew his whistle, signaling the birth of basketball. It is doubtful that Naismith envisioned future cheating scandals on that cold day in December 1891, but sadly, the game has seen its fair share over the years.

The Henry Hill and Jimmy Burke Debacle

Henry Hill, one of seven siblings, was welcomed into a working class life in 1943, when he was born in Manhattan to a Sicilian mother and an Irish father, both immigrants. Hill wasn't a good student and dropped out of school in his early teens to get involved with Varios, in various criminal activities. Paul Vario, his brother Vito, and his son Lenny involved Hill in illegal business, and at age sixteen, Hill was arrested for arson. In the years that followed his release, Hill would go on to fully immerse himself in mob business and graduate to stealing cars and hijacking trucks. He was in his mid-thirties when he became embroiled in what was dubbed the 1978–79 Boston College Basketball Point-Shaving Scheme.

Hill's associate was Jimmy Burke, a truly evil man, who allegedly orchestrated the biggest cash theft in US history (at the time) in 1978, "the Lufthansa Robbery." Burke is said to have killed his conspirators in the crime, but he was no stranger to murder. In 1962, he ended the life of his soon-to-be wife's ex-boyfriend and chopped him into pieces. Burke was a true gangster and enjoyed the protection of the Lucchese crime family, with which he was associated. By his standards, the Boston College Scheme was mild, but it did land him in prison for over a decade.

How Did It Happen?

Hill and Burke didn't actually come up with the scheme and were recruited later. The masterminds were the Perlo brothers, Rocco and Anthony. They weren't gangsters per se, but they were known in Pittsburgh for being "small-money" gangsters. Rocco was familiar with a Boston College player whom he was at school with and targeted him as a recruit prior to the 1978 season. Rick Kuhn was his name, and his task was to ensure that certain games finished within the points spread determined by the bookmakers.

The idea was to pick games in which Boston College was expected to win, but Kuhn couldn't do it alone, so he got his teammate and friend, Jim Sweeney, on board. The deal was lucrative, and essentially, going into business with the Perlo family was a no-brainer.

After all, there would be no need to throw games, which could be viewed as a plus for honesty. There is speculation as to whether leading point scorer Ernie Cobb was involved, the reason being that after the scandal broke, he accepted a fine but maintained that he had not participated.

In any case, the Perlo boys decided that they needed help from an influential gambler and chose a man by the name of Paul Mazzei, who had served time in prison with Henry Hill, and so the circle grew bigger. The scheme wasn't straightforward, which is why Hill brought in Jimmy Burke because of the latter's network within the larger gambling fraternity. Burke sourced bookies that had the resources to deal in large-sum bets and the ability to spread the bets widely among bookies around the country in a "hiding the odds in plain sight" way. The other bookies were unlikely to find out, but if they did, then the newly formed syndicate would deal with them, no doubt through threats of violence.

On December 6, 1978, the Providence Friars were pitted against the Boston College Eagles in the first of nine fixtures identified as fixable games. The plan failed miserably, as the Eagles won convincingly by 14 points more than the spread. In total, the execution of the plan was a failure, as the Eagles' players kept the score within the spread in certain games but failed to do so in others. Essentially, the scheme wasn't working, and the prior foreseeability of making good money did not pan out, so the gamblers made a call to end it, but not before one final fix.

The proposed fix was implemented in February 1979, when the Eagles faced the BC-Holy Cross. Kuhn and Sweeney were instructed to lose by more than three points; however, come the end of the game, BC-Holy Cross walked away with a 98-96 win. Sweeney, who had intentionally fouled out in the second half, was left high and dry, as the gamblers were left out of pocket and furious. That being said, the overall result of the whole scheme was that the syndicate was up, but not to the value that had been envisioned, and just like that, the scheme was over.

The Fallout

For some time, the players and gamblers would have thought that they were in the clear. After all, the scheme had run its course, and although it had not been as successful as hoped, there seemed to be no indication that anyone outside of the syndicate was aware of what had transpired. The rude awakening happened in 1980, and the exposure of the scheme had nothing to do with basketball.

Henry Hill was arrested for drug trafficking, after which it was revealed that he was heavily involved in the Lufthansa robbery, where almost $7 million was stolen at the JFK airport in New York. A state witness deal was struck, and Hill was granted immunity in exchange for confessing to all illegal dealings. The obvious result was naming names in the gambling scheme, and a trial ensued. Anthony Perla received ten years in prison, and his less-involved brother, Rocko, got four years. Kuhn, as the primary participating player, was initially sent away for ten years, which time period was reduced to under two and a half years. Paul Mazzei got ten years, while Jimmy Burke was sent away for twelve. Despite earlier admissions, Jim Sweeney was not charged at all, and Ernie Cobb was acquitted.

The Legacy

Although the points-shaving scandal was underwhelming in the end, the legacy of the gamblers' involvement and their ties to the mob is ongoing. The 1990 Martin Scorseese directed film, *Goodfellas*, inspired by Nicholas Pileggi's non-fiction book, *Wiseguy,* chronicled the life of Henry Hill's life of crime, mob activity, and gambling. Although a very minor focus of the book and film, the Boston College point-shaving scheme of 1978 and 1979 is immortalized to some degree. The scandal will never be forgotten, as its legacy transcends eras and remains talked about in living rooms, around barbecues, and in the stands at basketball games.

John "Hot Rod" Williams

The Cleveland Cavaliers star sadly died at the age of only 53, and despite his alleged but never proven involvement in bribery, he did a lot of good for the game. Hot Rod, so named for his propensity to make engine noises as a child, was somewhat of a slacker. He didn't put in much effort in the classroom and turned out to be a less-than-reliable member of Tulane University's basketball team. It can be argued that Williams was one of those athletes who got by on talent without commitment. When he graduated from college, his name was second on the list of all-time leading point scorers.

Alleged Tulane University Points Shaving Scandal

Although acquitted of all charges, Williams' NBA career was delayed in that he could not play in the NBA while he was still under indictment for bribery and conspiracy. The allegations were that Williams' and a teammate at Tulane were rewarded financially and with cocaine for shaving points in two games. The two players were arrested in 1985, after which Tulane scrapped its basketball program, forcing its athletic director to resign. It was an odd decision and may have pointed to guilt; however, the program was reinstated in 1989/90. The initial court inquiry was declared a mistrial, but a jury ruling of not guilty in the second trial meant that Williams was free to enter the NBA. He did admit to receiving game fees during his time at Tulane, as well as being paid an upfront fee of $10,000 upon enrollment. There was nothing illegal about this, but interesting nonetheless.

Professional Career

Williams was drafted from the Rhode Island Gulls by the Cleveland Cavaliers in 1985, but he spent the 1985-86 season with the Staten Island Stallions of the United States Basketball League. In the 1986–87 season, he joined the Cavaliers, and by the end of the season, he had been named to the NBA rookie team. The bench substitution specialist spent nine seasons with the Cavaliers before getting traded to the Phoenix Suns. William's successful career came to an end with the Dallas Mavericks. He advocated for better pay and signed a $26.5 million deal. An enormous amount in the early 1990s. Williams did not come without controversy, but ultimately he was an innocent man. In 2015, he passed away from colon cancer, but his legend still remains, even if things used to be a bit murky.

2007 Betting Scandal

Tim Donaghy, a professional umpire who enjoyed a 13-year career, was forced to retire in the wake of a gambling scandal. He umpired 792 games between 1994 and 2007. However, he is remembered more for his betting endeavors than his officiating.

How Did It Happen?

In December, a small-time gambler and longtime friend of Donaghy, James Battista, offered the legendary umpire $2000 per game to cover the spread. If he failed to do so, Battista would absorb the loss. A deal like that is too good to pass up, and Donaghy grabbed it with both hands. Battista was neither a gambler nor a bookmaker but rather a betting agent, called a mover. He would place bets on behalf of his clients with several bookies, some of them illegal but others not. Donaghy had the knowledge, and Battista somehow managed to be pre-funded by the sports betting underworld.

Battista involved an IT guy called Tommy Martino, whom he knew from school, as did Donaghy. To avoid any scrutiny, Donaghy used a burner phone to call Martino as soon as he was assigned fixtures to inform him of the pick. Martino would in turn contact Battista, ensuring that Donaghy and Battista never spoke. Battista would then begin placing bets for the majority of the day, and while this was never proven, rumors circulated that Battista would attempt to place bets worth $1 million from the bookmaker pals who were bankrolling him.

The plan was pretty damn simple, and Battista got on with the betting side of things. He reinforced the simplicity by referring to Donaghy as "the only mechanic he had in his hand." He had the "fucking whistle" and said directly to Donaghy, "You wanna get paid? Then you've got to cover the fucking spread."

The NBA conducted its investigation in 2007 and found that Donaghy had not fixed games, but questions were still being asked. Then in 2017, ESPN launched its own investigation. It was a major research operation that involved formal questioning of officials, players, gamblers, bookmakers, and lawyers. Donaghy himself chose not to be interviewed, despite several requests, but friends and relatives of the former referee did discuss matters with the investigating team. Court transcripts and documents were studied, and those involved painstakingly watched every game in the 2006–07 season that Donaghy had officiated in. The betting market line data for those games was analyzed, which meant that the investigation was fully comprehensive and left no stone unturned. The process took over two years, and the ultimate conclusion was that Donaghy had indeed conspired to fix NBA games.

Is There More to the Story?

Tim Donaghy was called up to the NBA after having officiated in the CBA for four years. For a 27-year-old in the big leagues in 1994, the pay was good, and the offseason afforded Donaghy a lot of time to spend his money. In 1998, Donaghy built a huge home adjoining a fairway at Radley Run, a country club of which he was a member. Radley Run was in West Chester, Pennsylvania, and its golf course was frequently used by Donaghy. He developed a circle of wealthy friends from the club, and along with Donaghy's school friends, they spent time playing golf, drinking, and gambling. The group frequented a casino in Atlantic City called Borgata, and later footage showed that Donaghy would always wear a cap pulled down to hide his eyes. The reason was that the NBA did not allow officials to gamble, and Donaghy did not want to arouse suspicion by being noticed.

One of the men in the group, called Jack Concannon, had a bookie named Peter Ruggieri, who was nicknamed "Rhino" due to his short and squat physique. Donaghy and Concannon decided to put their money together and bet on Ruggier's picks, an obvious violation of NBA rules. They experienced success in late 2002 and early 2003, so Donaghy and Concannon decided to take a step up and started betting on Donaghy's games, but they decided not to tell Ruggieri.

Like many schemes, it started slowly, but it got to the point where Donaghy was placing up to forty bets on games in which he was officiating. He was collecting so much cash that he struggled to find enough hiding places in order to ensure that his wife didn't start asking questions. James Battista, Peter Ruggieri, and some of their associates who had set up the online sports book, PlayASAP, discovered what was going on and promptly started betting on Donaghy-officiated games without telling the referee or Concannon. Battista and Ruggieri were onto a good thing and kept bets at a level where the larger bookmaking market would not catch on or suspect something nefarious.

The racket ran smoothly for a while, but in December 2006, Battista grew anxious that the betting markets were catching on. He made a panicked call to Tommy Martino, asked for a meeting, and explained everything, after which he asked Martino to set up a discussion with Donaghy. At that meeting, the "$2000 per game to cover the spread" deal was concluded. There have been slightly different accounts of who called the meetings and exactly what was said, but the point is that the deal was struck and that those involved swore to secrecy.

The Punishment

When the matter got to federal court in Brooklyn for the trial, the scenes were nothing less than pathetic. The professional gambler Battista cried excessively on the stand, as if he regretted his many years of illegal conduct. He was only crying because he was caught, and the judge saw right through it. Batista got a 15-month prison sentence for bets placed as a direct result of Tim Donaghy's tips. The middle man, Tommy Martino, also put in a performance not proportional to his persona and was sent away for 12 months.

Donaghy, who the judge called a pathological gambler, was sentenced to 15 months, to be spent at a facility in Pensacola, so he could be close to his four daughters. The humiliated referee was supported by a priest as well as his parents. He read what appeared to be a half-hearted apology and walked out of the courtroom grinning. Peter Ruggieri also got 15 months, but Concannon was never even charged.

Aside from the prison sentences, Battista and Martino were ordered to pay the NBA a joint sum of $217,266—about six times less than what the NBA asked for. Donnaghy was ordered to forfeit $30,000 in gambling winnings, but his lawyer, John Lauro, told the judge that he had already done so. There is no absolute confirmation on the amounts or whether Donnaghy did actually forfeit the $30,000, but the punishments can probably be said to be fair, although Concannon should count himself very lucky.

1949–1950 City College of New York Point Shaving Scandal

Around the time of this scandal, there was a widely held opinion among college basketballers that they should be getting paid. It wasn't an unfair argument, considering the hard work and commitment required to excel at the college level.

In 1950, the City College of New York Beavers had an excellent, well-drilled team that was using Madison Square Garden as a home venue. Coached by the legendary former NBA star Nat Holma, dubbed "Mr Basketball," he developed a playing style known as "the city game." The style was about creating shots through regular passing, fast dribbling up the court, and swiveling, allowing quick rotation of the ball. It was a new style and garnered attention, plus it changed the face of the game, which then developed into what we see today on the courts of the NBA.

CCNY had two starting African-Americans, which was very unusual at the time; in fact, the team was the epitome of diversity, including Jews, Italians, and Irish immigrants.

The team reflected the city of New York in its vibrance and acceptance. There happened to be an incident in 1950 involving the all-white Kentucky Wild Cats, who refused to shake hands with the CCNY players. The Beavers let their on-court play speak the loudest, and they thrashed the Wildcats by 39 points. CCNY faced Bradley University in the National Invitation Tournament as well as in the NCAA Division I Tournament and won both of the finals. Going into 1951, the Beavers carried a lot of expectations as another good season beckoned, but there was something amiss.

How Did It Happen?

We have to go back to 1949 to examine the start of the scandal, which was born in the Catskills, part of New York State's mountain belt. At the time, the Catskills had an array of summer jobs open to college students, but for athletes, the major motivation was basketball. Players would get involved in fiercely competitive games as entertainment for wealthy vacationers. The summer holiday games involved point shaving, but it was innocuous at first. A local chef who enjoyed betting with his employees secretly offered players free food for a week if they kept the score within a certain range. It was very rudimentary spread betting, and nobody got hurt or lost large amounts of money, so the consciences remained mostly clean.

After a short time, the points-shaving affair was greatly escalated by Long Island player Eddie Gard, who was connected with members of the Italian mafia and who spent holidays in the Catskills. Such a holiday-maker was Salvatore Solloazo, a dodgy-looking jeweler and petty criminal who was mainly involved in pool hustles. After a few discussions, a plan was hatched: Solloazo would create line bets on spreads and find anyone who would be interested. Gard did the rest, along with his teammates, as they did what they could to keep the score within the spread. It didn't work every single time, but Gard and his merry men were paid well when they were successful. Probably the biggest mistake that the fixers made was to bring the scheme into college basketball. The Catskills games, although competitive, weren't subject to any regulations and could have been said to be warm-up games, training games, or skill-honing games, so ramifications were non-existent.

Gard was greedy, and so was Solloazo; thus, the Long Island University player and his Italian pal got started in the NBA on January 17, 1950. The two men referred to "dumping" and "selling," being the dumping of points and selling of lines to bettors. Gard and two teammates ensured that the game was won within the line against North Carolina

University on January 17. Probably Long Island's best player at the time, Sherman White suspected something, as Gard's poor play was obvious, at least to White. He approached Gard to call him out, and soon enough, White was in on the scam. As one can imagine, it is not easy to completely control a game, and there were times when Long Island lost while trying to keep the winning score within the line.

The College Recruits

Word got around, and point shaving began to spread around the country. It was easy to talk college students into participating, as they were most often struggling financially, so Solloazo involved a connection that was not mentioned in the investigation. The man's name was Norm Mager, who played for the Beavers and recruited other players. Other schools showed the same pattern, and the fixing pot was fast boiling over, and by 1951, it could not be contained. On January 17 of that year, the first player arrests were made. Later, Solloazo, and Gard were arrested, with Sherman White being apprehended a short time later. The day prior to his arrest, White had been named Player of the Year by the *Sporting News Publication*.

The Punishment

Unfortunately, the losers were the honest players, as CCNY was banned from postseason competition and quickly fell from a formidable Division I team to an average Division III team. Madison Square Garden was out of bounds for CCNY, and the players involved in the scandal were barred from ever playing in the NBA. Sherman White was the only player who had a realistic NBA chance, so in addition to widespread embarrassment, his basketball career ended abruptly. It was a bitter pill to swallow, but the culprits had brought it upon themselves; the lesson was learned too late, but they got what they deserved.

The Fake Paralympians

This scandal is not only huge in paralympic circles, but it may be the biggest sporting scandal in sports history, simply because of the shameful and deplorable manner in which it was carried out.

The Plan

There isn't much to be said about the plan. A basketball team claiming to be mentally handicapped won Paralympic gold medals in the 2000 games held in Australia, only for the public to discover that certain players were not mentally handicapped.

The Big Reveal

The Sydney Paralympics concluded on October 29, 2000, and the basketball scandal was broken by Spain's Carlos Ribagorda in November of the same year. He claimed that other than the basketball team that he was part of, members of the track and field team, as well as the table tennis and swimming teams, were mentally sound. It was discovered that fifteen of the two hundred Spanish athletes competing in Sydney had no mental handicap. Ribagorda further stated that he had been a member of the team for two years prior to the paralympics, even though medical and psychological reports showed that he was not mentally or physically handicapped. It turned out that only two of the twelve Spanish basketballers were considered mentally capped, due to IQ tests revealing scores of less than seventy, which placed them into the category of mentally handicapped. The remaining ten players relied on fake medical certificates as proof of disability.

Spain's first game in the 2000 Paralympics was against China, and when Ribagorda broke the scandal, he alleged that the Spanish coach had told the team to "gear down" when they were up by thirty points.

The beginning of the end was the team's celebrations after "winning" gold against Russia in the final of the basketball tournament. Photographs were published in a Spanish newspaper called Marca, and the public recognized local players who were certainly not disabled in any way.

Martin Vicente, head of the Spanish Association for Mentally Handicapped Sports, resigned just after the truth was revealed. Vicente had full knowledge of the whole scandal and, upon his departure, announced that he took full responsibility. There was an outcry as to how full responsibility did not garner immediate sanctions, and Spanish public opinion was that it was water off a duck's back for Vicente.

Sport, Like Life Is Unfair

The team was stripped of their medals and the sport of basketball for intellectually disabled individuals was no longer included in the Paralympic program as a result of their punishment. It's hardly fair to legitimately handicapped players all over the world.

Vicente received a pathetically insufficient punishment, comprising a fine of €5,400 ($4,860) and an order requiring him to return €142,355 ($128,120), the amount of the subsidies received by the federation for athletes without disabilities.

The entire scandal was disgusting, as cowards took advantage of aspirant winners, over whom they had a clear advantage. Punishment was completely inadequate, and the world of paralympic sport was the loser in the end. One cannot help but bear a heavy heart upon hearing the story, except for Vicente, of course.

Chapter 3

Football/Soccer

Whether you call it football or soccer, there is no doubt that it is a truly global game, played in 226 countries on fields, roads, squares, dusty sand patches, and even indoors. Although games vaguely resembling football as we know it today have been traced back more than four thousand years, the "beautiful game" was officially sanctioned in 1856. In the annals of history, soccer is said to have originated in England, but several other countries claim to have had influence on its invention. That is neither here nor there. Soccer has produced legends over the years, from Pele to Maradona to Ronaldo, Ronaldinho, Messi, and Cristiano Ronaldo. The game has also produced some legendary scandals, but soccer has remained resolute. No matter how many scandals have taken place and will take place in the future, the game will never lose its popularity.

Italian Soccer Scandals

The 1980 Totonero Scandal

Dubbed the Totonero Affair, this fiasco involved Avellima, Bologna, Lazio, Milan, Perugia, Palermo, and Taranto. The first five clubs were part of Serie A, the top tier of local Italian soccer, and the last two were part of Serie B, the second division. Paolo Rossi is remembered for two things. The second of the two was the way in which the striker helped Italy to a World Cup victory in 1982, breaking a 44-year drought. During the World Cup, he scored a hatrick against Brazil, which helped him finish the tournament as the top goal scorer. He became an instant Italian legend, along with the rest of the 1982 team.

For the first reason, we have to go back to the Serie A season in 1978–79, where the Perugian striker scored 13 goals and assisted the club in reaching the last 16 in the UEFA Cup. The scandal ran deep and involved illegal Italian gambling schemes, which fell under investigation upon receiving information in March 1980 that games were being fixed. The informants were two shopkeepers in Rome who came forward and said that Italian players had been asking for money to throw matches. Arrests were made en masse, and players received differing multi-year bans according to their level of involvement. The five Serie A teams were relegated, and the two Serie B teams were each docked five points.

Switching back to 1982, Rossi's ban was shortened so that he could play in the World Cup, and just about every Italian had forgotten about the match-fixing scandal. Rossi had a formidable presence on the soccer field and seemed to lift his teammates to create great performances. It could be argued that he deserved stricter punishment; however, no such actions were taken, and that is the end of the matter. Rossi remained a national hero, even after his passing in Siena in December 2020.

The Calciopoli Scandal of 2007

The plan in this scandal wasn't particularly complex, but that did not mean that the culprits would get away with it. In simple terms, members of the Juventus Football Club got referees to influence the outcomes of games for an agreed-upon wager. It started when the club's general manager, Luciano Moggi, teamed up with the club chairman, Antonio Giraudo. Moggi had become friends with the head of UEFA's referee committee, Pierluigi Pairetto, who agreed to allocate referees involved in the scandal to Juventus fixtures. The scheme didn't work very well, as Juventus lost in the quarter finals of the UEFA Champions League in two consecutive seasons.

Milan, Fiorentina, Lazio, and Reggina were also involved, but not to the extent that Juventus participated. When the scandal broke, a comprehensive investigation took place, involving 41 alleged participants. 33 games were meticulously reviewed, and by the conclusion of the investigation, all five teams were found guilty and handed point deductions. Lazio and Fiorentina, who had qualified for the 2006–2007 European competitions, were forced to withdraw as part of their punishment. Luciano Moggi was banned from all football for a period of five years. Prosecutor Stefano Palazzi made an example out of

Juventus, who were stripped of their titles. Along with their forced demotion and points deduction, they began the next season's Serie B season on nine negative points.

Not only did the punishment embarrass the club and put them in a position where it would be difficult to compete, given what was essentially a handicap, but over thirty Juventus players left the club. Two huge names, Zlatan Ibrahimovic and Patrick Viera, moved to Inter Milan, and the Romanian forward, Adrien Mutu, went to Fiorentina. Real Madrid also hired Juventus manager Fabio Capello. He took Brazil's Emerson Ferreira and Italy's Fabio Cannavaro with him and left Juventus in a position that looked like it would take several seasons to recover from. It was not the case, and they cruised through the Serie B season, securing promotion with a 5–1 victory against Arezzo in May 2007. The whole fiasco was a black smear on the club's history, but they put it behind them quickly as they climbed the Serie A ranks once again. Sadly, the club did not learn its lesson.

Mafia Influences on Match Fixing

Italy is a country of soccer fans who identify with each other through the national sport, which transcends generations, socio-economic groups, and prejudices. However, in the past ten to fifteen years, crime has become part of the game that the public loves so much. The Calabrian Ndrangheta became associated with Juventus managers in 2019, with the 2007 Calciopoli scandal all but forgotten. This faction of the Italian Mafia is dominant throughout Europe and several other countries in the world. With murder, high-speed chases, mass drug movements, and a history of kidnapping, this oversized gang of fear mongers is not to be messed with!

A ruling from the Supreme Court in April 2019 concluded that the 'Ndrangheta controlled a system where Juventus managers secretly supplied free tickets to the mafia men. The tickets were passed on to the most extreme of Juventus supporters, 'Ndrangheta controlled a system where Juventus managers secretly supplied free tickets to the mafia men. The tickets were passed on to the most extreme of Juventus supporters, the "ultras," who sold the tickets to fans. The ultras are known for football hooliganism and their rejection of any form of rule, so it wasn't difficult to involve them. Everyone must get paid, so the manager and the ultras received compensation for their participation. One could argue that they were being ripped off by the Ndrangheta, but money is money, and this loot came for free.

Return to 2018 and the story of Vincenzo Iaquinta's firearms offenses. He delivered guns to his father, who was subject to a court order prohibiting him from possessing weapons. Iaquinta senior had been associated with the 'Ndrangheta for several years, and his involvement in the gun running fiasco landed him in prison for 19 years. The trial involved 148 people, roughly 120 of whom were found guilty of various offenses and were accordingly sentenced. Strangely, Iaquinta Junior received no jail time.

The Italian football industry turns over €2.3 billion ($2.49 billion) annually, but the actual figure is much higher, considering the large amounts of money that are generated through the many illegalities. Having said that, the 'Ndrangeta engage in legal, if shaky, endeavors in order to increase their own prestige. The endeavors include providing finance for the development of youth soccer and sponsoring young players. One could argue that power and influence are the results, but not credibility or integrity. The situation is largely a "turn a blind eye" culture, and there are ongoing investigations into the mafia across all activities and even other sports by special committees.

As one can imagine, the mafia has a vast network of contacts. As an example, consider Giuseppe Sculli, the son of an almost lifelong mafioso and Italian international. While playing for Genoa in 2012, a gang of home-supporter ultras showed their displeasure after halftime of a game against Siena in 2012, when their team was 4–0 down (Cripps, 2014). About 80 of the ultras made their way to the players' tunnel just after halftime and started chanting, setting off flares, and throwing fireworks onto the field. Their demands to have the game stopped were met after 20 or so minutes of play, and Sculli was involved in a physical altercation with one of the ultras.

Sculli was touted as a hero when Corriere Dello Sport, a national Italian newspaper, called the incident "a chilling spectacle...right out of the dark ages." Sculli said that he drew his bravery from his grandfather, Giuseppe Morabito, which is probably a stupid thing to say, considering the mob affiliation.

Sculli did not live up to the promise he showed as a teenager in the football world. In addition, he was caught up in other scandals. His rap sheet includes an eight-month ban for fixing a match between Crotone and Messina. As part of a group of players, Sculli fixed games along with members of Lazio, Lecce, and Genoa, only to be placed under investigation again. The court found that Sculli had suspicious meetings with

Domenico Criscito and Safet Altic. The former was an Italian international and the latter a known Bosnian criminal, both of whom were known match fixers. The meetings were to discuss extorting professional footballer, Luca Toni, who was said to have been behaving inappropriately with other women while his wife was pregnant. Sculli was cleared, but the whole affair just added to his tarnished reputation.

Despite all the scandals in which he was involved and his ties to the mob through his grandfather, Sculli enjoyed a 16-year career, including an Olympic bronze medal. When you step back and look at the situation, you realize that his career was always going to be entwined with questionable behavior and reputation-damaging illegalities; it was just the life of a man who couldn't get away from controversy.

German Soccer

The Danish Football Association selection team was responsible for a victory on German soil over the Hamburg-Altona Football Association. In fact, it was a 5–0 thrashing, but to be fair to the Germans, they did not have country-wide representation. The fixture was in mid-April 1897, but the first recognized international match in German football history was against Switzerland, 11 years later, on April 5, 1908, in Basel; Germany lost 5–3.

German football was underwhelming over the years and was not well funded. They were unable to attend the first Football World Cup, held in Uruguay in 1930, largely due to the great depression. The German national team did, however, qualify for the 1934 World Cup, where they finished third. The next major event for the men from Germany was the 1936 Olympic Games, where they failed to impress.

As one can imagine, the national team was affected largely by politics over the years, and at one point during World War II, all international games were suspended due to the mandated army conscription. Sanctions imposed on the three German states at the time—Saarland, East Germany, and West Germany—meant that no internationals took place until 1950.

Saarland was seceded by France and is no longer part of the said states. Various internal competitions took place in East and West Germany, which both maintained complete separation. As the game evolved, semi-professionalism turned into professionalism, and the Bundesliga was formed in mid-1963. The separate states reunified in 1990, and German football continued to strengthen. The national team won their first major competition after reunification when they defeated the Czech Republic in the Euro 1996 final. Ever since, Germany has been a major force in world football, but we have to jump back to 1971 to examine what was an enormous match-fixing scandal in the Bundesliga.

The 1971 Bundesliga Match Fixing Scandal

Horst-Gregorio Canellas, the then-director of Kickers Offenbach, was the most prominent figure involved. The Kickers, a Bundesliga club, play out of the state of Hessen and have had a history of promotions and relegations, but they are best known for the events that took place in 1971, a season that saw Offenbach finish one place off the bottom of the table. The team had looked out of sorts, making mistakes unbecoming of professional footballers, and eyebrows began to be raised. The story broke when Canellas made an obvious press release about the secrets that he was carrying. A whole lot of shadiness, bribery, dishonesty, and match fixing happened in the lead up to that press conference, though, and so, back to the start.

What Went Down?

Arminia Bielefeld, currently a Division II Bundesliga team, was the main team in a scandal of huge proportions. The Bundesliga players were semi-professional and in the Bundesliga in 1971. Relegation loomed, and that meant that the club would most likely fall apart as the players would not be able to supplement their work earnings through football. The "very close to the camel's back breaking straw" was when Bielefeld lost 5–0 to Kickers Offenbach and had to come up with a plan, so they sent one of their full-time professionals to Schalke. Waldemar Slomyani, a Bielefeld midfielder, convinced some of the Schalke players to throw the upcoming match between the two teams. The first man to agree was up and coming forward Klaus Fischer, but the seniors were more difficult to persuade, though once they realized how simple it was to throw a football match, many of them agreed.

Bielefeld's end of the bargain was to do a wire transfer to Schalke before the game. The amount was 40,000 DM ($19,900), not a large sum of money but significant enough for Bielefeld, whose woes were not only performance-based but also financial. It must have been a toss-up, with the decision being that the amount was a good enough investment to prevent relegation and risking the collapse of the club. Schalke accordingly threw the game on April 17, 1971, and Bielefeld took the first step towards avoiding relegation. The fix nearly backfired when Schalke's first-choice goalkeeper was injured and his replacement was unaware of the plan. Dieter Burdenski, the back-up keeper, was playing to win, but when Schalke player Stan Libuda was somehow told by someone in the Bielefeld camp that should Schalke win, the money would have to be returned, Libuda informed Burdenski of the plan. A collective sigh of relief was let out by the Bielefeld men as the Schalke team realized how easy it was to fix a game. Fans, spectators, and punters put it down to laziness and complacency. Thoughts of a fix were far from the minds of the greater Schalke fraternity, and football carried on unabated.

Around the same time, unbeknownst to Schalke, Bielefeld had widened the fix, when they paid Essen, a North Rhine-Westphalia team, to lose to their neighbors, FC Koln. Then Essen jumped on board by bribing their compatriots, Rot-Weiss Oberhausen, also from North Rhine-Westphalia. The whole fiasco was becoming ridiculous, and FC Koln was the next team to accept money to throw a game, this time against Oberhausen. Stuttgart were next on Bielefelds list, and a 1–0 fixed match saw Bielefeld needing one more victory to avoid a relegation tragedy.

When Bielefeld got Hertha to take a bribe in exchange for the fix, their goalkeeper, Volkmar Gross, got clever—and greedy. The Hertha pitcher claimed that Kickers Offenbach had offered him 160,000 deutsche marks to ensure a loss, and Bielefeld put 250,000 deutsche marks on the table. Either way, a Bielefeld win was all but guaranteed, and the result was 1–0. The Hertha crowd was livid and verbally ushered their players off the field with chants of "Bribe! Bribe! Bribe!"

Bielefeld successfully avoided relegation, but Rot-Weiss Essen and the Kickers found themselves down in the 2. Bundesliga. A day after the final relegation game, Horst-Gregorio Canellas blew German internal football wide open as he revealed the entire scandal to the salivating, lip-licking press.

The Fallout

A major investigation was set underway, and other alleged fixers started popping up all over the place, some guilty, some innocent. At first, the entire Schalke squad denied any involvement or knowledge. The denials were made under oath, and one young player was put in a very difficult position. Lie and play football, or tell the truth and be banned. The player was Klaus Fischer, Schalke's all-time leading Bundesliga goal scorer. In 1971, he d hungry for a successful football career, so when his seniors told him to lie, ...d just that.

The entire investigation took ebbs and flows, during which punishments were handed out, as it meandered along until 1976, when Fischer, on the stand in a district court, pleaded guilty to bribery and perjury. Both offenses ordinarily carried prison time, but neither Fischer nor anyone else involved saw the inside of a jail. The German authorities reported that the reason for bypassing the laws was due to "special circumstances." Fischer and the other men must have considered themselves lucky, especially since there was no record of any foregoing of a due prison sentence in German history as a result of "special circumstances."

Nearly all the Schalke players were banned from German football for a year, and several were banned from the national side for five years. 29 players from the other clubs involved received bans, as did several managers and directors. The player who perhaps suffered the worst overall result was Hertha's keeper, Volkmar Gross. His ban kicked in prior to the 1974 World Cup, which Germany won. It is hard not to be empathetic considering the match he threw was a dead rubber and the outcome was inconsequential for Hertha, but cheating is cheating.

Players and clubs were also subject to large fines, but time was the biggest price for Klaus Fischer, who lost five years of possible international football. Considering his achievements and legendary status, one can only imagine what he would have done had he been able to play during those five years. Still, Fischer will always be remembered as the second best, behind Gerd Muller, who shone during Fischer's five years of absenteeism. The biggest losers were Kickers Offenbach, who currently reside in the Bundesliga's fourth tier, but none of it had to happen. The reality, though, is that it did happen, on a large scale, and the big fixing scandal tarnished the Bundesliga.

Bundesliga Match Fixing Scandal

Granted, this scandal took place in the second and third divisions of German football and was not on the scale of the 1971 fixing fiasco; however, it involved some serious money and, this time, a prison sentence. Ante Sapina, a footballer from Croatia, and his two brothers, all heavily involved in sports betting, orchestrated a €2 million ($2,3 million) betting operation. Referee Robert Hoyzer was the first recruit and was soon joined by Dominik Marks. Hoyzer ended up turning on Marks by going public and testifying against his fellow official. Games played between May 30, 2004, and December 3, 2004, were scrutinized. Hoyzer received bribes in nine of those games and Marks in four of them, while several others were declared as clean. The most obvious Hoyzer fix was when he ensured that Paderborn, the regional league side, knocked out first division team Hamburg in the first round of the German Cup. As an aside, Paderborn played out of North-Rhine-Westphalia, the city in which two clubs from the 1971 scandal were from. In the 2004 Cup fixture, Hamburg were leading 2–0, when Hoyzer awarded two dubious penalties and sent Emile Mpenza back to the dugout for what looked like an innocuous tackle. Ante Sapina and his brothers allegedly made around €750,000 ($900,000) on the game, and another €870,000 ($1,04 million) on a second division game thanks to Marks' purposefully questionable officiating. Hoyzer walked away with €67,000 ($80,000)and Marks with €36,000 ($43,000). A scant reward considering the money that Sapina made.

Marks got off lightly with an 18-month suspended sentence, as did Ante Sapina's two brothers, who got 12- and 16-month suspended sentences, respectively. Ante was sentenced to 35 months in prison, while Hoyzer was sentenced to 29 months. At a later stage, Steffen Karl was fingered for his part in the Paderborn game and was found guilty of purposefully underperforming. His sentence of 9 months was suspended, but he did receive a 6 month ban, which ended German football's second biggest scandal. Lesson learnt? Maybe, maybe not.

French Football Bribery Scandal

Marseille's football club has a long history of success, especially in domestic competitions. They lifted the French Cup for the first time in the 1923–1924 season and have since won another 10 titles. They have also been multiple French Ligue 1 champions. Despite domestic success, the men from Marseille have only won the European Champions League on a single occasion, in 1992–1993. Although it is believed that the final against Milan was free of bribery, the final match of the French Ligue I season, less than a week before the Champions League victory, was most certainly a fix.

The Tainted Victory

The French Ligue I title hung in the balance, with Marseille needing a victory away to Valenciennes. Marseille won 1–0 and claimed the title, but something seemed wrong. The Valenciennes players appeared out of sorts, and their play was uncharacteristic. It surfaced at a later stage that Valenciennes' defender, Jacques Glassman, opened his mouth during the half-time break, telling coach Boro Primorac that he had been offered money to throw the game. The offer had come from Jean-Pierre Bernes, Marseille's director, and Glassman's former Nantes teammate, Jean-Jacques Eydelie. Club director Bernard Tapie had overseen the entire operation as part of his obsession with winning.

On June 8, 2003, a criminal investigation began, which uncovered further offers. Christopher Robert and Jorge Burruchage, of Valenciennes, had been approached to help with the fix. Robert's wife collected the reward in the Marseille team hotel's parking lot, and it was later buried in her mother's garden.

The Aftermath

There were calls for Marseille to be stripped of their Champions League title, but it never happened. The disgraced club was banned from the Champions League the following season and unceremoniously dumped out of Ligue I domestic football. Both Tapie and Bernes received partially suspended prison sentences. The former served eight months and the latter only three weeks. Jean-Jacques Eydelie was banned from football for 18 months and jailed for 17 days. Marseille was hit hard financially and declared bankruptcy, but was able to pull itself back into Ligue I in 1996. Marseille have not won a major European event since 1992–1993, and one has to wonder if the Valenciennes scandal tarnished the powerful French team.

The Floodlight Failures Betting Scandal

This scandal was a unique one that didn't last long, and examination of the modus operandi shows proof that it was not sustainable. It could also be said that it was a pretty stupid idea.

What Happened?

Wai Yuen Liu, a Hong Kong-born Londoner, along with two Malaysian associates, Eng Hwa Lim and Chee Kew Ong, paid a security guard to fiddle with the floodlights at a football game. The purse was £20,000 GBP ($33,000), and the task given to the guard was to allow access to the floodlights for the installation of a device that could shut off the lights using a remote control. The three crooks wanted to have a match at The Valley, Charlton Athletic's home ground, but it was cast into darkness and thus abandoned. This scheme was run by Far Eastern betting syndicates, which worked with huge amounts of money. If a game was abandoned for any reason after halftime, bets were not returned. Timing was important, which did pose a small risk. The ideal situation would be for the favorites to be down, or even at halftime, then to shut down the lights shortly into the second half and to claim amounts allegedly in the tens of millions from bets following the odds.

The Charlton game was played in February 1998, and they defeated Liverpool by one goal to nil. The lights were never cut, the reason being that a few days before the game, the security guard, Roger Firth, let out the secret. Liu, Lim, and Ong were arrested in the parking lot of the stadium before the fixture, and obscene amounts of money were lost by the Hong Kong Triads. There had been other incidents the previous season where floodlight "failure" had occurred. A particularly memorable "floodlight failure" happened in November 1997, shortly after Frank Lampard (Jnr), playing for West Ham, scored an equalizer against Crystal Palace at Upton Park. One would have to turn a serious blind eye to conclude that the prior games, such as the Hammers versus Palace match affected by the lights, were not part of the same scheme.

The Punishment

Roger Firth and the two Malaysians pleaded guilty to conspiracy to cause a public disturbance. Firth was sentenced to eighteen months, with Lim and Ong each receiving four-year sentences. Liu pleaded not guilty but was unsuccessful and was put away for thirty months on the same charges as the other three men.

The Ghost Game Phenomenon

Creating ghost games and fake games is tricky, but bookies had a run where they successfully made money by exploiting the scam. The way it works is that companies that collect data for bookmakers are given listings of games that don't ever take place, i.e., ghost games. Fake games are slightly different; they are games that take place but that are played by different teams than the ones listed.

The Perfect Ghost Game Scam

In late March 2020, a fictitious tournament was created in the Ukraine, and the listings were supplied to bookies across the world. There were four lower-league teams in the fictitious tournament. It was called the Azov Cup and was "promoted" vaguely on social media. The data feed was provided by a company called Bet Genius, and the data was supplied as real and live. All the fixtures were completed before the cover of the non-existent tournament was blown.

The Reveal

On March 27, 2020, the Ukraine Football Association publicly stated that they had come across knowledge that the games were fake and that they were created to scam betting markets. The fraudsters neglected to take into account the isolation due to the COVID-19 pandemic, meaning that teams were not even practicing, let alone playing. Bet Genius came forward with an apology to its customers. There was little to no investigation, and no names were given, but there are suspicions that the culprits were Turkish or Belorussian. Pockets were lined without accountability or punishment, making it a perfect scam, but maybe with time, more detail will be revealed.

Paying Out on a "Friendly"

The "friendly" took place in Belarus, where Shakhter Soligorsk were beaten by FC Slutsk in the non-existent game. Sbobet was the company that paid out, as the two Belorussian teams denied any involvement. Shakhter Soligorsk alleged that their website had been hacked. No person, football club, or bookmaker was investigated in this 2015 incident, and it may have been a one-time payday before the parties responsible got out.

Moving the Goalposts

In this case, the sporting saying "moving the goalposts" is not just a metaphor. It actually happened. What makes this endeavor even more baffling is that the culprit, Kim Christensen, did this in 2009, by which time there were cameras all over the place. The Dane, who was playing for IFK Gothenburg at the time, was caught on camera moving the goalposts before a game against Orebro. The referee was notified about twenty minutes into the first half, and moved the posts back. After the game, Christensen admitted to having done it before, but it garnered little further attention, and he went on to represent Denmark in one 2010 fixture before retiring from professional football in 2018.

The Hand of God

Whether you see him as a hero or a villain, there is no denying that Diego Maradona was a charismatic, bombastic, heart-on-sleeve man. From tax dodging to cocaine and alcohol abuse to controversial political views to firing air rifles at journalists, Maradona has been involved in many off-field controversies. However, he is remembered most for his involvement in arguably the most infamous on-field incident in football history. To many, the man was a god, and as the world watched the 1986 Football World Cup quarter final between Argentina and England on June 22, Maradona did something that only a god could get away with.

The Man, the Legend

Known as "El Pibe de Oro," meaning "the Golden Boy," Diego Maradona, at age fifteen, became the youngest ever player in the Argentine Primera División when he donned the number sixteen jersey for Argentinos Juniors. Five years, 167 games, and 115 goals later, he moved to Boca Juniors. Maradona, who had grown up poor, was barely out of his teens when he left Boca Juniors for Barcelona Football Club, after signing a then-world record $7.6 million contract. The Golden Boy already had a World Cup under his belt, but in the 1982 edition, Argentina didn't live up to their billing. The South Americans failed to make the last 16, but Maradona would go on to play in another three World Cups. In 1990, he had been at Napoli for five seasons and led the Argentine national side to the final, where they were defeated by West Germany. During the 1994 tournament, he left with a cloud over his head after testing positive for a banned substance and never played international football again. The drama, however, occurred during the 1986 World Cup.

Mexico, '86

The Falklands War between England and Argentina overlapped the World Cup. an unlikely conflict, where Argentina invaded the Falkland Islands, as well as South Georgia and the South Sandwich Islands, in an effort to reclaim what they asserted to be Argentinian territory. The war lasted barely three months, with Argentina surrendering eight days before the World Cup quarter final clash against England, so perhaps there was a cross to bear. In the group stages, Argentina claimed two victories, against Korea and Bulgaria, respectively, and a draw against a powerful Italian outfit. The men from South America finished top of their group and downed Uruguay in the round of 16 to face England in the quarter finals. In their pool game against Portugal, England lost 1–0, but a 0–0 draw against Morocco and a convincing 3–0 win over Poland saw England finish second in their group. Paraguay were next and got a 3–0 thrashing, handing England a quarter final berth.

The final score was 2–1 in favor of Argentina, and Maradona scored both goals. The second one was probably the best goal of the World Cup. The Golden Boy, from just inside his own half, pivoted with the ball at his feet and broke away with speed. As he ran down the right flank, he beat defender Terry Butcher on the inside, then Butcher's namesake, Terry Fenwick, on the outside. Maradona seamlessly entered the box and netted the ball mid-tackle. He was on his feet almost immediately, to be greeted by an ovation from over one hundred thousand screaming fans.

Goal two was talked about for all the right reasons, but it was goal one that raised overwhelming controversy. Maradona made a searing run up the middle of the field, easing past Glen Hoddle, then made a dash towards the box, laying the ball off to forward Jorge Valdano, front right. Valdano couldn't maintain control, and Steve Hodge threw a boot out, sending the ball looping into the penalty area. By that point, Maradona had darted into the box, flung himself into the air, and tipped the ball over the oncoming England keeper, Peter Shilton. On his left side, the Golden Boy turned and ran towards the crowd.His teammates followed, and wild celebrations from players and spectators alike ensued. It was a confusing situation, especially considering that replays and photographs studied after the game convincingly showed that the ball was handled. Maradona was quoted as saying that "it had gone a little with the head of Maradona and a little with the hand of God." Argentina went on to dispose of Belgium in the semi-final with the help of two Maradona goals. Although he didn't score in the 3–2 victory over Germany in the final, his tournament statistics were incredible. The Golden Boy played every game from start to finish, scoring five goals and assisting on five others.He was named player of the tournament, and the Azteca Stadium, in which the final took place, erected a statue of Maradona scoring the second goal, with the inscription, "Goal of the Century."

Nineteen years later, Maradona put an end to still-raging debates by announcing that he had indeed used his hand. Maybe he got away with it because he was Maradona, or maybe it was a terrible refereeing mistake. In any case, football punters around the world will never forget the Golden Boy, who died in November 2020. It is fascinating that he scored one of the best goals in World Cup history and the undisputed most infamous goal in World Cup history in the same match.

Chapter 4

Cricket

The so-called gentleman's game has had its fair share of controversial incidents, such as the bodyline series in the early 1930s between Australia and England. Douglas Jardine instructed his English troops to bowl directly at their opponents' bodies. These tactics had never been seen before, and deliberately trying to hurt your opponents caused a huge outcry. Then there was the occasion in 1979 when Australia's Dennis Lillee attempted to use an aluminum bat, which damaged the ball. He was confronted by the English opponents and instructed by the umpires to use a wooden bat. Dennis Lillee threw the aluminum bat about twenty meters in a moment of anger, and despite calls for punishment, nothing was done. In 1981, Trevor Chappel's underarm ball to New Zealand's Brian McKechnie secured Australia's victory. In addition to McKechnie's countryman, Richard Hadlee, kicking crowd favorite Pakistani all-rounder, Imran Khan, in the shin, and West Indies' Michael Holding, booting a stump out of the ground in disgust after a bad umpiring decision.

The above incidents pale in comparison to the early etchings of match fixing, when Pakistan's Saleem Malik was first caught. The door had been opened, and Hansie Cronje walked right through it, participating in cricket's biggest ever match-fixing scandal and taking several teammates down with him. Since then, cricket has had some tough times, but its status as the second most popular sport in the world also ensures the dirt is forgotten quickly.

The IPL's Darkest Days

The Indian Premier League was the catalyst for the unprecedented exchange of large sums of money in cricket. The tournament was conceived in 2007, with the first edition being played in 2008. Eight empty teams, called franchises, were named and sold to billionaire business people and Bollywood stars. The total spent was over $720 million; an auction followed, where the best players in the world were bought, and the teams took shape. Indian superstar MS Dhoni was bought for about $1.14 million by the Chennai Super Kings in the first auction. Not a bad payday for five to six weeks of cricket. For the first time, cricketers were earning ridiculous amounts of money, and for the team owners, it was business. The IPL did wonders for world cricket, but pockets were lined and controversies were revealed.

The architect of the IPL, Lalit Modi, a rich and successful businessman, was charged with financial misgovernance and corruption in 2010. The then-IPL chairman was immediately dismissed. Modi had been abusing his privileges by awarding tenders to family and friends. In 2013, the Board of Control for Cricket in India (BCCI) handed Modi a lifetime ban. The cricket-loving public didn't care; it was a boardroom scandal, not a cricket scandal.

Spot-Fixing

The structure of cricket games is such that bets can be placed on certain amounts of runs being given away by a bowler in a specific over or on a batsman getting less than a specified amount of runs. To achieve either of these feats is easy; the bowler just needs to bowl a series of bad balls that any half-decent batsman would score off. In the case of a batsman, all he has to do is lose his wicket on purpose by purposefully missing the ball, running himself out, or dishing up an easy catch. The simplicity of the plan and the monetary rewards are thus very tempting—just ask Shanthakumaran Sreesanth.

30-year-old Shanthakumaran Sreesanth had racked up 27 test appearances for India. Suffice to say that he carried a fair amount of influence, especially over Ajit Chandila, who was contracted to IPL franchise Rajasthan Royals during the 2013 IPL season, as was Sreesanth. Although the two men were close in age, Chandila, in comparison with his countryman, had very little top-level cricket experience, which made him an easy target as a spot-fixer. A third member of the Royals squad, originally from Mumbai, Ankeet Chavan, was also involved. He too didn't have the kind of experience or influence that Sreesanth had, and in addition, he wasn't making the kind of money that his nationally capped compatriot was making.

Sreesanth was then arrested by the Delhi Police, along with fellow Rajasthan Royals players Ajit Chandila and Ankeet Chavan, in addition to eleven bookies. The players were charged with spot-fixing and suspended pending an investigation. The Rajasthan Royals' team personnel put out a statement condemning the players' alleged activities.

A few days later, Vindoo Dara Singh, a well-known actor, and a man by the name of Gurunath Meiyappan were arrested by the Mumbai Police. The latter was a former Chennai Super Kings (CSK) team principal and the son-in-law of the head honcho of the BCCI at the time, N. Srinivasan. Considering the family connection, the might of the BCCI, and the wealth of Singh, the charges of betting and links to bookies made sense. Investigators examined telephone records and discovered that Singh and Meiyappan were in frequent contact. CSK immediately cut ties with Meiyappan, and questioning by the Mumbai Crime Branch ensued.

The authorities discovered that Meiyappan had a discussion with Stephen Fleming, CSK coach, about strategic changes to the batting order prior to a game before giving the information to Vindoo Dara Singh, who fed it to the bookies. On that same day, N. Srinivasan announced that the scandal may have involved family members but that he would not be stepping down. When the BCCI disciplinary commission was set up to undertake a full investigation, requests came from the top brass asking that Srinivasan be distanced from the commission.

There was a comical side, in that Ankeet Chavan made a successful application for special bail so that he could attend his own wedding on June 2, but he was back in jail on June 6. Four days later, he was granted bail once more, along with Sreesanth and seventeen other related arrestees, while the third Rajasthan Royal, Ajit Chandila, did not apply for bail.

The BCCI secretary, Sanjay Jagdale, and its treasurer, Ajay Shirke, resigned immediately. Rajeev Shukla, the IPL chairman, left his post, as did Srinivasan, but only temporarily. Indian cricket was in turmoil, and the Delhi Police were not taking investigations lightly. Raj Kundra, co-owner of the Rajasthan Royals, was next; he was questioned about placing bets through a bookie known to the Royals. Team management reacted quickly and promised to recall all of Kundra's shares in the franchise and suspend him if the allegations were proved to be true.

Meanwhile, a promising young cricketer and member of the India Under-19 international team, Harmeet Singh, was linked to a Mumbai spot-fixing incident. Ravi Sawani, head of security at the BCCI, got Singh to put forward all the information he had regarding the involvement of the three Royals players. Singh, who had played one game for Rajasthan, complied and recorded a statement revealing all that he (allegedly) knew.

A lot of back and forth ensued, as committees were appointed, then de-commissioned, however Kundra, along with the Royals co-owners, and the CSK owners were cleared of any wrongdoing. On 30 June 2013, the Bombay High Court ruled that the committee that cleared the two IPL giants was illegally created, and furthermore that the entire investigation be started over.

After the conclusion of the fresh investigations, Sreesanth, Chavan, and Chandila were cleared of all charges, but the Rajasthan and CSK owners received two-year bans. Gurunath Meiyeppan and his father-in-law, N. Srinivasan, were found by the Justice Mukul Mudgal Committee to have shared information and placed bets together on fixed IPL games.

Supporter attendance was not affected, as stadiums around India carried on selling out tickets. Viewership on television suffered a fourteen percent knock, but a circus as huge as the Indian Premier League did not take long to recover. With multinational companies such as CEAT Tyres, the Tata Group, and PayTM pouring billions into the tournament, it is no wonder that the IPL has maintained its popularity. The 2013 scandal, although big at the time, is of no consequence now. The IPL is still loved and supported in droves as the players increase their bank balances significantly, the team owners revel in the excitement of the popularity contest, and the world watches the best of the best go head-to-head for two months, every year without fail.

The Pakistan Cricket Spot-fixing Scandal

It can be argued that Pakistan's Saleem Malik was the first cricketer to draw widespread attention to match fixing in the late 1990s. Malik was handed a life ban in 2000 after he was found to be in collusion with bookies on a major scale in several fixed games. Jump forward ten years and the Pakistanis were at it again; the Malik incident was not enough of a deterrent, and the 2010 spot-fixing scandal provided proof thereof.

Pakistan was playing an away series against England, and in the fourth test match at Lord's Cricket Ground, the visitors started bowling some very suspicious no-balls. Little did the cricketing world know, but the weekly tabloid publication, News of the World, had been doing some behind-the-scenes investigating. Its reporters had managed to secretly film Mazhar Majeed, a man who called himself a "sports agent" and was counting bribe money. In the video, Majeed can be seen confirming that Pakistan's pace bowler, Mohammad Amir, would bowl a no-ball first delivery in the third over. Majeed also stated that the sixth ball in the tenth over would be an illegal delivery, this time delivered by Mohammad Asif. The two Mohammads did indeed bowl no-balls, but Amir's was so big that the likelihood of it being a genuine mistake was very low.

Mohammad Amir made his Pakistan debut in a test match in Sri Lanka during a 2009 tour. He was only seventeen and touted as a fiery quick bowler with a promising career ahead. His co-conspirator, Mohammad Asif, was a five-year veteran of Pakistan cricket by the time the England tour came around. Team captain Salman Butt, who played a total of sixty-eight tests for Pakistan, was also named for his involvement. Then president of the Pakistan Cricket Board, Ijaz Butt (no relation to Salman), rubbished the allegations, claiming that his players were innocent, and there were rumors from former players that it was a set-up. Then the politicians got involved, and the Pakistan National Assembly called for the players to be sacked. Rather, the three accused were suspended by the International Cricket Council (ICC). Appeals were filed, and as is the case in these situations, there were postponements, which dragged the whole thing out.

On February 5, 2011, the ICC reached a decision banning Butt for ten years, with five suspended. Asif received a seven-year ban, with two suspended, and Asif got five years. In November of that same year, Mazhar Majeed was handed down a two-year, eight-month prison sentence, while Butt got two years and six months. Mohammad Asif got one year, and the youngster Amir got off lightest, with six months. One may argue that Majeed was lucky, but perhaps the punishments for the players were too harsh. Perhaps some people feel that prison time is not appropriate for cheating and that the shame and international embarrassment are enough punishment. Those questions remain unanswered, but it can be said with certainty that the careers of the players were severely affected.

Hansie-Gate

Wessel Johannes Cronje, known as "Hansie," was the darling of South African cricket until a match-fixing scandal made him sports villain number one. South Africa has a dark history of racism and violence under the Apartheid regime. Whites were treated as first-class citizens, and non-whites were kept separate, with suppressed rights and poor living conditions. In 1970, the rest of the world imposed sports sanctions on South Africa, meaning that no international competition was allowed across the board. Twenty years later, Hansie was soon to be the South African cricket captain as the country was readmitted into international competition. Through sport, South Africa was brought together with the fall of apartheid, and Hansie led the charge on the cricket field.

The Match-Fixing Scandal

1996 was the year during which Hansie Cronje met Mukesh Gupta, a dodgy bookmaker. Cronje had a brief taste of match fixing the previous year, when he was offered $10,000 to throw a One-Day International (ODI) against Pakistan. Cronje refused on that occasion, but the promise of easy money must have occupied his thoughts for some time, as he was quick to accept Gupta's offer of $30,000 to purposefully lose wickets on the final day of the third test away against India. The offer was facilitated through Mohammad Azharuddin (not to be confused with Mohammad Azharuddeen), an Indian international batsman who scored an impressive twenty-two test centuries during a ninety-nine test match career. Interestingly, Cronje didn't tell his team or ask any players to throw the game, as South Africa were bound to lose anyway by the time he received the offer. He didn't know it yet, but Cronje had been drawn into an underworld from which he would never escape.

While still on tour in India, Cronje was offered a whopping $250,000 to throw the final game, a dead rubber ODI. On December 13, 1996, the day before the ODI, Cronje called a team meeting. In the meeting, Cronje explained the offer, but the team declined to accept it. On December 21, 1996, as part of India's reciprocal tour to South Africa, a three-day warm-up match took place between the visitors and a domestic outfit, Eastern Province. There was nothing untoward in that game, but come December 26, the first day of the first test, held in Durban, on South Africa's east coast, Cronje had accepted $50,000 from his new betting friend. Gupta was in South Africa at the time, and in exchange for the money, Cronje was required to give Gupta information about team selection for the first test and, later, about South Africa's intended declaration in the third test. Gupta had also offered Cronje $300,000 to throw the final test, but the South African skipper refused.

In the future, it would be revealed that Cronje had an obsession with money and also an obsession with accumulating rather than spending. His sister, Hester Parsons, was quoted as saying, "He was such a cheapskate, he was always giving away his freebies for Christmas and birthday presents." Cricketers didn't earn the kind of money back then that they do now, but international players were most certainly earning enough to buy Christmas presents.

It was in a test match against England in South Africa, played on the highveld at Centurian Park, when things became outrageous. The test had been subject to a lot of rain, and come the final day, Cronje did something that no cricket team had ever done. He forfeited an entire inning to "make a game of it," and the South Africans posted 249, which England chased down. Even though South Africa had lost, Cronje was lauded as a tremendous athlete for giving England a chance and for providing entertainment to a disappointed crowd. Not everyone was convinced, and talks of a fix started getting some coverage. Indeed, it was a pre-planned loss; Cronje had done it for money and nothing else.

Marlon Arenstam, a crooked South African bookie, had asked Cronje if he would make the unprecedented move of giving England a realistic winning chance. For his involvement, Cronje was rewarded with 50,000 South African Rands ($11,300), which paled in comparison to his previous USD payments. Arenstam would describe the money and a leather jacket that he gifted Cronje as "down payments" for future betting fixes.

Next up was India away and multiple telephone conversations with Sanjay Chawla, a bookmaker who was under investigation for non-cricket-related matters. As part of the investigation, Chawla's phone was bugged, and the Delhi Police were inadvertently put into the match-fixing loop.

Cronje claimed in future years that he was attempting to "string Chawla along," but that Chawla's relentless pursuit of Cronje led to the South African captain caving again. That was probably not true, especially since Cronje offered bribes to teammates Herschelle Gibbs and Henry Williams. Gibbs, an explosive opening batsman, was instructed to give away his wicket for less than twenty runs in exchange for $15,000. Williams was offered the same amount to intentionally bowl poorly and give up a large number of runs Cronje was in for a shock, as Gibbs scored seventy-four and Williams suffered an injury in his second over and could not continue. Cronje lost out big time, allegedly ten times the amount that he was going to pay Gibbs and Williams. In fact, Cronje had told Chawla that the two youngsters had requested $25,000 each, which was not the case. Cronje was planning to keep the extra $20,000,

The Fallout

Hansie Cronje's world came crashing down on April 7, 2000, when Delhi police charged him with match-fixing. On April 9, 2000, Cronje lied to the cricketing world as he denied everything during a special press conference. Exactly two months after Cronje was charged, the King Commission, set up by the then president of South Africa, Thabo Mbeki, and chaired by Justice Edwin King, got underway. Herschelle Gibbs admitted to his proposed involvement but explained that he had not gone through with it and did not receive the $15,000 The same was the case with Henry Williams, and the two players were fined in addition to receiving a six-month ban.

On June 15, 2020, Hansie Cronje read out a lengthy statement on the stand in front of Justice King. It is believed that Cronje did not disclose the full details of the amounts received, but the discovery that he had over seventy Cayman Island bank accounts suggested that the scheme was intricate enough to hide a fair amount of detail. The last line of Cronje's statement proved hauntingly poignant, as the disgraced cricketer said, "as long as there is gambling on sporting events, legal or otherwise, players will continue to be approached, pressured, and tempted."

Cronje was banned for life in October 2000 but died less than two years later when a light aircraft in which he was traveling slammed into the Outeniqua mountain range in South Africa. Two other crew members also lost their lives, and a probe into possible foul play followed. It was found that nothing nefarious occurred and that the crash was due to pilot error. Cricket lovers the world over were left in a state of shock, but there was a sense that Cronje's death was timely, not as a punishment for his criminal activity but as a pardon to relieve him of his pain and regret.

The Mervyn Westfield Controversy

In a Durham versus Essex clash in the 2009 county cricket season, the latter's Mervyn Westfield set out to bowl poorly on purpose, allowing the Durham batsmen to score freely. His bounty was £6,000 GBP ($9,800), but his efforts earned him a four-month jail sentence.

Westfield, who was twenty-one at the time, claimed that Dinesh Kaneria, a former Pakistan international, had pressured him to take part. It may have been the case, but at the hearing in London's Crown Court, Justice Anthony Morris was of the opinion that Westfield had ample opportunity to speak to his captain, or management, or at the very least, his teammates.

The scandal might have been revealed anyway, but Westfield shot himself in the foot when he showed a senior teammate, Tony Pallidino, the wads of money that he had received. Pallidino did not keep Westfield's secret, and at the hearing it was discovered that Kaneria had two years prior been given an official warning by the ICC's anti-corruption unit over suspicions of dealings with an unnamed bookmaker. In the Westfield case, Kaneria was released without charge in 2010, but did admit to his involvement in 2018, after nine years of denials. After Westfield's release, he faded into the abyss and had only himself to blame for wrecking his career.

The Bob Woolmer Mystery

The likable former England cricketer and South African national team coach was found dead in his Kingston, Jamaica, hotel room during the 2007 ODI World Cup. Woolmer was only 58, and his premature death came as a shock to the cricket world, especially since the circumstances were very strange indeed.

Woolmer had taken over the position as Pakistan coach from the seasoned Javed Miandad in 2004 and enjoyed considerable success over the years to follow. Come the 2007 World Cup, Pakistan and the man at the helm, Brad Woolmer, were touted as favorites to win the tournament. The Pakistani team was eliminated from the World Cup in the group stages after a disappointing performance against the much less fancied Ireland team on March 17, 2007. At the press conference that followed, when asked if he was going to resign, Woolmer did not answer yes or no. Sadly, Woolmer never got the opportunity to answer that question, as the cricket world awoke to news of his death on March 18, 2007.

Bertram Carr drove Woolmer and his men back to their hotel that night, and the silence was overwhelming, only broken by bouts of coughing from Woolmer. The somber Pakistani coach had one drink with his former opponent, Ian Gould, at the hotel bar before going to his room. Later that evening, Woolmer sent an email to his wife, Gill, saying that he was feeling terribly disappointed and telling her that he loved her. Woolmer didn't show up for breakfast the next morning, alerting suspicion, and at around 10:30 a.m., a maid found Woolmer's lifeless body in the bathroom. It wouldn't have been untoward to presume that Woolmer died of some sort of health complication, taking into account that he was diabetic and had sleep apnea. A half-eaten lasagna and an empty bottle of champagne were found in his room, but nothing suggested foul play.

Whodunnit?

The post-mortem could not conclusively determine a cause of death, and on March 22, journalists claimed strangulation. The Jamaican police swiftly released a statement saying that the pathologist had indicated that Woolmer's death was due to strangulation and that a murder case had been opened. There was deliberation among the ICC about potentially abandoning the rest of the World Cup, but in the end it was allowed to continue.

The man appointed to spearhead the aggressive probe into the matter was Mark Shields, Deputy Commissioner of the Jamaican Police, whose CV included investigations into the Irish Republican Army, international money laundering rackets, and the Russian mafia. Shields seemed to revel in the attention, but he had the experience and was the best man for the job.

Various theories from journalists and punters started doing the rounds, one of which was that Woolmer was about to drop a truth bomb, admitting to his involvement in the Hansie Cronje match-fixing scandal. It was rumored that Woolmer had information on rampant Pakistani cricket cheating, ball tampering, and religious rifts within the squad, which he was set to reveal. Sarfraz Nawaz, a former Pakistani cricketer and politician known for his controversial statements and eccentric behavior, was of the opinion that Woolmer was killed by, as he put it, "the match-fixing mafia." Nawaz went on to suggest that Pakistan had thrown an earlier pool game against the West Indies, safe in the (false) knowledge that they would progress into the next round by winning their games against

Ireland and Zimbabwe. Another consideration was that Pakistan were overwhelming favorites against Ireland, so a shock result could have been planned in exchange for big money. It had happened before, many times, and could realistically have happened again.

The chief investigator, Shields, felt that there was no doubt whatsoever as to foul play. There were rumblings about an email sent by Woolmer to the Pakistan Cricket Board chairman in the early hours of his final day alive. Nothing came of the rumblings, but journalists started having a field day with claims of poisoning and then strangulation. Suddenly Shields went dead quiet, and it appeared that he had prematurely jumped to conclusions, as the spotlight fell on the pathologist, Dr. Ere Seshaiah. He had grown up in India and qualified with an M.D. in forensic medicine from the Sri Venkateshwara Medical College. Although Sheshaiah had not met all the requirements to be appointed state pathologist, his twelve years of experience made him an expert in the field. The same opinion was not shared by three independent pathologists from three different countries, and Seshaiah admitted in a later inquiry that he had made a mistake in his initial findings. During his testimony, Seshaiah added poisoning by insecticide but maintained strangulation. However, an independent senior forensic laboratory expert from Jamaica confirmed the presence of the insecticide, which he described as "significant."

The inquest was led by lawyer-turned-coroner Patrick Murphy, and as per Jamaican law, the final decision would be reached by Murphy and the jury of eleven. Thanks to John Slaughter of the London Forensic Science Service and Professor Tara Dasgupta, a pesticide researcher at the University of the West Indies, more confusion occurred. Both experts concluded that no traces of poison were present in Woolmer's blood samples. The jury concluded that there was not enough evidence and too many inconsistencies to find in favor of murder or natural causes. An anticlimactic ending, which leaves the question open forever, but a sad story nonetheless.

The Underarm Bowling Incident of 1981

In an ODI at the Melbourne Cricket Ground (MCG) in the summer of 1981, the crowd saw something that had never been seen before in a professional cricket match. Australia was facing New Zealand in the final of the World Series Cup, which consisted of five games in total. On February 1, when the third match started, the two teams were tied at 1–1. The Melbourne game swayed back and forth, and on the very last ball of the day,

New Zealand needed six runs to tie the game. If a six was hit, then the entire game would be replayed on another date.

Trevor Chappel was the bowler, and Brian McKechnie was the batsman. The odds of McKechnie hitting a six were low, but to be safe, Trevor's older brother and team captain, Greg, instructed him to bowl an underarm ball. It is impossible to hit a rolling ball for six, and all McKechnie could do was block the ball. The frustrated New Zealander threw his bat in disgust, and immediate shame was cast upon Chappell. Quite ironically, Ian Chappel, the eldest of the brothers, was commentating on the game and was clearly appalled. Richie Benaud, an Australian broadcasting legend and former player, called the incident disgraceful and classified it as one of the worst things that he had ever seen on a cricket field.

Bowling underarm was actually within the rules but was severely frowned upon, and an unwritten rule was in place that underarm deliveries were never bowled. Even in school games and social leagues, underarm balls simply did not happen; they were not even thought about.

The outcry was loud and scathing as the New Zealand and Australian Prime Ministers offered their public opinions. The former called the Australian players cowards and labeled the incident "disgusting." His Australian counterpart classified the infamous delivery as an act contrary to the traditions of the game.

The Chappells, and the Aftermath

The rule was changed, and underarm balls were officially written out of the game by the ICC. The Chappell brothers issued public apologies and articulated their embarrassment, but Trevor never shook his legacy as the perpetrator of the 1981 incident. With time, the memories faded, and McKechnie held no grudge. In fact, there have been many humorous recreations of the event during benefit games and even in television advertisements.

One can safely say that although the infamous underarm ball was against the spirit of the game, it was a mild manipulation of the rules when compared with the rampant and brazen match-fixing scandals that shocked the cricketing world in years to come.

Chapter 5

American Football

American football initially developed as a cross between rugby and soccer in the mid-nineteenth century. At the time, there was no fixed set of rules, so depending on where the game was played, the rules would differ. The first official college football game was played in 1869 between Princeton and Rutgers University, in New Jersey, using a modified set of association football rules. Other universities followed with their own rules, but in 1873, all the colleges that played the game now known as American football met to establish one set of standardized rules. Harvard refused to attend the meeting and kept its own rules, but in 1876, a final set of rules was agreed upon across the board, based primarily on rugby. In 1880, there were also agreed-upon rule changes, one of which was a reduction in players from 15 to 11 per team. As the early twentieth century progressed, the sport started to become more popular and enjoyed widespread attention.

Over the years, professionalism developed, and players were paid in exchange for their on-field services. By 1920, players had started moving from professional team to team based on the best monetary offers, including college footballers while still registered at university. The game required some sort of regulation, and thus the American Professional Football Association was born. In 1922, the National Football League (NFL) was formed. In 1960, the American Football League (AFL) was created, which became a rival to the NFL. In 1970, the AFL and NFL merged to form the NFL as we know it today, consisting of 32 teams from the American Football Conference and the National Football Conference. Unfortunately, the pure intentions of the sport back in the nineteenth century have not always been upheld by players, coaches, and outside influencers, leaving a trail of dishonesty, gambling, and cheating.

The Alex Karras and Paul Hornung Controversy

Alex Karras certainly had a privileged upbringing, along with his two older brothers, both of whom were professional footballers, just like Karras. The youngest of the siblings was the most talented in other sports. He was a track star and a promising high school wrestler, but his first and ongoing love was football. Karras, unlike modern-day players, spent his entire professional career with the Detroit Lions, between 1958 and 1970. A truly diverse man, he appeared in 22 screen titles on television and on the big screen. In addition, he published a journal detailing his time with the Lions, as well as a memoir and a novel. As Karras grew older, his health suffered, and he died of kidney failure in October 2012. He had dementia by that point, which was thought to be the result of numerous concussions during his 12 year professional football career. When he passed away, he was held in high esteem by those who knew him well and by those who did not know him. However, there was a serious black mark from illegal gambling in his past that will be talked about for the rest of football's existence.

Paul Hornung, also a talented all-around athlete, got involved in the same activities as Karris. Hornung's professional career wasn't quite as long. He spent seven years with the Green Bay Packers and one offseason with the New Orleans Saints. During his time at Notre Dame, Hornung demonstrated versatility to the point where he was regarded as the best all-around footballer the school had ever produced. He won the coveted Heisman Trophy in 1956, prior to beginning his pro career in 1957. Like Karras, Hornung experienced mental difficulties in later life after suffering many concussions during his playing days. He died in Louisville, his beloved hometown, in 2020; cause of death: dementia.

The Scandal

Hornung first. The man enjoyed gambling, but perhaps calling him addicted would be going too far. One of his betting joys was horses, and although his dream was to own a horse that would run in the Kentucky Derby, he never quite managed it but came close. Other than horses, Hornung bets on college football games and NFL games too. He claimed that he only ever bet on the Packers to win, and popular opinion suggests that it was not a lie.

In 1959, Vince Lombardi took over at the Packers, which coincided with Hornung's career taking off as well as his gambling. His wagers were placed with a San Francisco-based associate, and it wasn't small money either. The running back continued placing bets until he was caught in 1963. He didn't try particularly hard to hide his endeavors. Pete Rozelle was the man who confronted Hornung, and the latter made no denials. Rozelle acted as the commissioner of the NFL for almost 30 years and did a tremendous amount for the game. After discussing the matter with Vince Lombardi, a decision was made to suspend Hornung for one season, with the reason cited as "gambling and associating with undesirables."

A few months later, the same fate befell Alex Karras, who had been warned several times that betting was against the regulations. Initially, no actual allegations were made, but with time, it was discovered that Karras had placed five, maybe more, $100 bets. This was enough for Pete Rozelle to issue a one-season suspension to Karras, who was furious. He believed that.

Hornung was more remorseful and made more than one public apology. There was something about the way in which Hornung conducted himself, gracefully and bashfully accepting his punishment, that didn't leave the public upset for too long. The two men had both done wrong, but one developed a strong resentment for Rozelle, and the other developed respect on the basis that Rozelle had done the right thing.

The Calvin Ridley Saga

Some may say it was unfortunate; others may say it was deserved. Ridley's professional career was cut short due to his suspension for gambling. Ridley made his NFL debut for the Atlanta Falcons against the Philadelphia Eagles in 2018, shortly after signing a four-year deal worth just short of $11 million. Over the next four seasons, Ridley excelled in his role as wide receiver, so much so that the Falcons gave him an $11.1 million contract for the 2022 season. Ridley did not see any of that money. He had to forego the whole amount due to his indefinite suspension imposed on March 7, 2022. Although indefinite, the mandatory minimum time out of the game would be until the end of the 2022 season.

The Fallout

There was a deafening public outcry and the strong suggestion that betting should be permitted, in light of the fact that the NFL has lucrative gambling promotion deals with sites like Fanduel. The general opinion appears to be that if players bet on their own teams to win, then there is no problem. It was probably of no consequence, but the five bets placed in November 2021 were made while Ridley was taking a brief hiatus from the game due to mental health issues. Ridley was open about the bets that he had placed and used Twitter to offer his take on the situation. One tweet read, "I bet 1500 total and I don't have a gambling problem," which he followed up with a second tweet, saying, "I know I was wrong, but I'm getting 1 year lol." The tweets were obvious indications of his dissatisfaction with the punishment. Ridley was completely compliant with the investigators, who were informed of the gambling by a compliance company contracted to the NFL. The bets were placed legally on a legal betting app without any inside tips or other information whatsoever.

Roger Goodall, NFL Commissioner, stated that gambling was one of the most, if not the most, serious violations of the sports code of ethics. Considering that it was not cheating, it was not done illegally, and it was not done in a backhanded manner, the punishment could be said to be too harsh.

A school of thought emerged, where the contention was that domestic violence by players garnered six-game suspensions, even though the infraction is way more serious than betting on one's own team. One of the players to receive a six-game suspension was Adrian Peterson. He was indicted in 2014 on charges of reckless or negligent injury to a child, and in 2022, he was removed from an airplane due to an altercation with his wife that led to a domestic violence charge.

Domestic violence can never be condoned. However, on one side of the coin, it has nothing to do with football and is the domain of the courts. On the other side of the coin, gambling on football is directly related to football. Either way, at the time of writing, Calvin Ridley is still under suspension, and he will have to see what awaits him.

The Full Brian Flores Investigation

Brian Flores, of Honduran descent, was robbed of a professional career by injury, although he did enjoy a four-year stint as a player at Boston College. The next best thing was coaching, and even though he began as a scouting agent, Flores became a coach of acclaim who experienced much success, including four Super Bowl championships. Unfortunately, 2022 saw allegations of tanking made against Flores, which led to a six-month investigation by the NFL. Mary Jo White, SEC Chairperson and former U.S. Attorney, aided by lawyers from the firm Debevoise, conducted the inquiry and reported the findings to NFL Commissioner Roger Goodell.

The investigation had to determine two things, and I will quote directly from the Goodell report (2022):

Whether the Dolphins violated League rules prohibiting tampering with a player and a coach under contract to other clubs. Whether, in the 2019 season, the Dolphins intentionally lost games to improve the club's draft position in the 2020 draft, and whether Dolphins' chairman and managing general practitioner, Mr. Stephen Ross, offered head coach Brian Flores financial incentives or otherwise encouraged him to lose games.

The Facts and the Findings

In 2019 and 2020, Tom Brady was under contract with the New England Patriots, while he was in regular communication with the Miami Dolphins. Such communications were impermissible but semi-disguised, as Brady did not deal with Stephen Ross directly. His point of contact was Bruce Beal, a potential future owner of the Dolphins. Beal would then talk to Ross, explaining the details of his discussions with Brady.

The impermissible contact spilled over into 2021, at which time Brady was contracted to the Tampa Bay Buccaneers. This time, both Ross and Beal were directly involved in discussions with Brady. It was tabled that Brady may be given the option to move to the Dolphins as a player or possibly an executive. His name was thrown into the ring as a possible candidate for a limited partnership in the franchise.

As 2021 became 2022, Ross and Beal started talking to Don Yee. These communications were also not permitted, but Yee, the agent of the New Orleans Saints' head coach, Sean Payton, was neither bothered; nor concerned about being caught. The topic discussed was a potential contract being handed to Payton as head coach of the Dolphins. A short while later, Payton resigned from the Saints, at which point the Dolphins requested permission to enter into discussions with Payton. The Saints refused, and investigations would later reveal that the duration and extent of the discussions had never been seen before. The potential detriment to other teams was unprecedented, but the question of whether or not the Dolphins tanked games in 2019 had not yet been answered.

As the investigation progressed, there did not appear to be any witnesses or conclusive evidence that the Dolphins had played to lose. Similarly, Ross was absolved of the accusation that he imposed pressure on Flores to engage in tanking. The fact that the Dolphins had beaten Cincinnati and the Patriots towards the end of the season worked against the accusers. Had the Dolphins lost those two games, their position in the draft would have been much more favorable, meaning that the tanking allegations logically must have been false.

During the season, Ross emphatically stated on more than one occasion that improving his position in the draft would never be placed above winning. Those listening to Ross' assertions were the team's CEO, Senior Vice President, and Brian Flores. The frequency with which Ross made these comments was unsettling for Flores, and it is understandable that Flores thought that Ross was trying to hide something. It was almost as if Ross was trying to deny something without being accused of it first. Flores allegedly wrote to the senior executives, putting his views forward, after which Ross never raised the subject again with Flores.

Something peculiar about the investigation was a finding that Ross had offered to pay Flores $100,000 to play tank games but that the offer was not a serious one. This was a misnomer because the subject should not be something that is joked about, but nonetheless, the findings could not be argued.

The competence of the investigators was called into question, especially considering that the punishments did not seem to fit the crimes. They were as follows:

- The Dolphins were ordered to forfeit their first-round selection in the 2023 draft and their third-round selection in the 2024 draft.
- Ross's suspension was extended until October 17, 2022. During the period of suspension, he was barred from being present at the Dolphins' facility or at any

team or NFL event. In addition, Ross was removed from all league committees and fined $1.5 million. Ross is a billionaire eleven times over, so it's not a big financial hit.

- Bruce Beal was banned from attending any league meeting until the end of 2022 and was fined $500. Similar to Ross, the financial punishment was almost insignificant, taking into account Beal's family net worth of approximately $10 billion.

There seems to be something amiss, or something that doesn't tie up; maybe in years to come, we will discover that there is more to the tale than we have been led to believe.

The New England Patriots, and "Spygate"

It was a young man named Matt Estrella, with a relatively innocuous job at the Patriots, who was responsible for revealing the scandal known as "spygate." He didn't reveal it on purpose, but he was caught capturing defensive signals by the New York Jets' assistant defensive coaches. Estrella was a video assistant, and at only 26 years old, he was an easy target to do the dirty work, as instructed by his seniors in the Patriots camp.

Filming opposition coaches is not completely prohibited, but the problem in this case was that Estrella was capturing the signals from outside the allowable area. In fact, his camera operation was taking place on the same sideline as the Jets' coaches.

The very first accusations surfaced at a fixture between the Patriots and the Jets, in New Rutherford. At the time, there was no way of knowing if there was credence to the accusations, which were made by Eric Mangini, the Jets' coach, against Bill Belichick, the man in charge of the Patriots. Mangini might have held back if he had known the gravity of what would ensue, but once the cat was out of the bag, it was not going back in. It seemed as if Mangini felt bad, guilty, or a combination of both because he tried to play it down in an apology statement.

The sanctions that followed were harsh, as the Patriots were slapped with a $250,000 fine. What's worse is that the New Englanders were stripped of their 2008 NFL Draft first-round picks. The situation could have been worse if the team failed to make the play-offs, in which case their second- and third-round picks would have fallen by the wayside.

It turned out that the Patriots did get into the playoffs. Belichick received $500,000 but was lucky not to be suspended.

It was the same NFL commissioner, Roger Goodel, that oversaw matters, and in addition to the fines and draft penalties, he ordered that any and all playbooks, notes, and tapes be handed over to the NFL commission. There is no way of knowing whether the Patriots held anything back, but it was announced by Goodell that everything they received was subsequently destroyed. A tape somehow surfaced on Fox's NFL Sunday, but time frames indicated that there was nothing untoward—interesting nonetheless.

The matter appeared to have come to a close when a man named Matt Walsh, who was a previous Patriots' employee, leveled further accusations going back to 2001, before he was suddenly sacked in 2002. Reading between the lines, it seemed as if Walsh was told to shut his mouth by the Patriots, and there was talk of a confidentiality agreement that he was coerced into signing. Discussions between the NFL and Walsh began towards the beginning of March 2008, with the goal of signing an agreement indemnifying Walsh from any adverse legal or financial damages that may result from the contents of a proposed interview. Nothing had been finalized by the end of March, when Robert Kraft, owner of the Patriots, came out with a bizarre comment, saying that he did not remember Walsh as an employee of his team and that no confidentiality agreement had been signed. Yes, the staff at an NFL franchise team is large, but in light of the situation, one would have expected Kraft to have at least known of Walsh.

After continued discussions, the NFL announced on April 23 that an indemnity agreement had been reached with Walsh and that a meeting between Walsh and Roger Goodell would be scheduled to discuss the matter further. Walsh was requested to send the tapes that he still had in his possession to the NFL five days before the meeting, which would take place in New York on May 13, 2008. Walsh provided eight tapes made at six fixtures in 2000, 2001, and 2002, and on the set date, a marathon meeting took place at the NFL headquarters. Various lawyers and officials were also present, meaning that it was probably a daunting task for Walsh.

Arlen Specter, a congressman who had previously been cynical about Goodell's ruling that all playbooks, notes, and tapes were to be destroyed, requested a meeting with Walsh the next day in Washington, D.C. Subsequent to the meeting, Specter issued a statement in which he talked about a 2002 game between the Patriots and the Pittsburgh Steelers. He said that Walsh had general admission credentials and wore his Patriots jersey inside out. There was little clarity as to the truth of the statement, but also confusion about what point Specter was trying to make.

In an interview with the New York Times on May 15, Walsh revealed that he and senior video director Jimmy Dee had brainstormed alibis that could be used if allegations of impermissible taping surfaced. At some point, Walsh expressed his surprise that Belichick did not have a recollection of him, and in what was becoming an arguably irrelevant mudslinging exercise, Belichick accused Walsh of exaggerating. In an interview with CBS News, Belichick talked about how he and Walsh "did not have much of a relationship" (Keteyian, 2008). The intimation was that "not much of a relationship" was an indication that there was at least some form of a relationship, meaning that Belichick must have known Walsh.

Specter jumped back in and called for an independent investigation. Before it could take place, other senators called him out for focusing on a frivolous issue in comparison to real issues affecting Americans. The Democratic Party's Ted Kennedy, a fellow congressman and seat holder on the judiciary's Senate Committee, vociferously conveyed that football was for entertainment, but that the Iraq war, the continued impoverishment of U.S. households, and the skyrocketing gas prices were significantly more important than a few men and their cameras. Specter accepted the criticism and announced that he would not pursue any further investigation by the Senate. And so the storm in the proverbial teacup died off very quickly, leaving the public with a "don't care" attitude. However, the NFL has not been able to shake off the strange nature of the whole scandal, but the game continues, and the public continues to support their beloved sport.

Tom Brady, and "Deflategate"

If you thought that Brady's only controversy was the secret discussions with the Miami Dolphins in Bruce Flores' case, you would be wrong. Deflategate, however, took place back in 2015, in an American Football Conference title encounter. Brady was well over ten years into his professional career with the New England Patriots when the scandalous fixture against the Indianapolis Colts took place.

Some may say they love Brady; others may not feel that love, but there is no denying that he is an excellent quarterback, probably the best that has ever played the game. He had a sterling college career, and an even better pro career having won seven Super Bowls and five MVP accolades. At the time of this writing, Brady is still playing in the big leagues at age 44. He is a legend of the game, but a tarnished one.

Deflategate, the Speculation

The inflation rate, measured in pounds per square inch, is regulated between 12.5 and 13.5. At the time of the alleged deflation in the Colts game, the NFL did not record the inflation levels prior to the game. Logically, the pre-game testing was thus redundant. Dean Blandino, currently a Fox Sports analyst, but the vice president of the NFL Officiating Committee during deflategate, was the man who revealed that the levels were not recorded. There wasn't necessarily a reason; it was something that was never thought about. As long as the footballs complied with the regulation, they were allowed to be used in games. Considering that somewhere between twelve and twenty balls are used per game, there is certainly room for hidden deflation. In the Colts game, it was alleged by Ian Rappaport of the NFL Network that eleven of the twelve balls allocated to the Patriots were below the allowable level when tested at halftime. The purists, or "blind-eye-turners," put forward science theories that called on temperature pressure as a factor that affects pounds per inch levels. A poor argument, one would say. The strange thing was that balls had never been tested at halftime, raising the question of why this suddenly occurred. Did officials know something? Were they tipped off? Was there a vendetta against the Patriots? difficult questions to answer, but in the wake of the testing, a dragged-out investigation started.

Who Was Involved?

A 253-page report found that Brady was, to quote directly, "at least generally aware." That was of course not the only conclusion; there was a lot more to the story, but some of the findings were vague, to say the least. John Jastremski was, at the time, an equipment manager for the Patriots. He acted along with Jim McNally, who was also involved on the equipment side. The report found that the two men were involved, and again, to quote directly, "it was more probable than not that they were an integral part of the plot." Again, a pretty vague statement, but more specifically, the report set out that there was a one minute and 42 second time period during which McNally deflated the balls in the bathroom prior to kickoff. At this point, the report got more detailed. During the investigation, a scientific firm was contracted to undertake a study, the results of which led to the conclusion that the time period was sufficient for an individual to use a needle to deflate the balls. It was recorded that there were thirteen balls in total, although it seems as if only eleven were used during the game.

At a later stage, McNally said that he would regularly take footballs to the bathroom before games. It seemed a strange thing to do, and an equally strange thing to make public, especially as part of a denial. The report set out text messages between McNally and Jastremski, in which McNally called himself "the deflator." The NFL appointed an attorney, Ted Wells, who studied the evidence before compiling the report. Wells found that the text message could not possibly be ignored and amounted to conclusive evidence of the alleged misconduct. During discussions between Wells and the two equipment men, they denied everything and classified the messages as jokes. Given the gravity of the situation, this is not something to laugh about. Furthermore, Brady's telephone call logs were scrutinized by Wells, and he discovered that multiple lengthy conversations between Brady, McNally, and Jastremski took place during the Deflategate saga. The actual call recordings and text messages could not be accessed because Brady destroyed his phone prior to the investigation. Unfortunately, the evidence could only be called circumstantial, but the self-same Roger Goodell, who went on to investigate Brady in the Spygate saga, called the phone destruction "a wilful obstruction of justice." Brady, while under oath, told Wells and the commission that he regularly gave mobile phones to various assistants to be destroyed. Wells opined that it appeared as if Brady was trying to hide something and that he may be guilty, but the lack of evidence on the mobile phone front limited Wells to an opinion only.

The Punishment

The New England Patriots were given a $1 million dollar fine, and Brady was suspended for four games by the NFL. The rulings were made on May 11, 2015, and three days later, an appeal was lodged by Brady through the NFL Players Association. On June 28, 2015, Roger Goodell, who noted that Brady had been uncooperative, denied the appeal. The Players Association then approached the U.S. District Court for Southern New York, and Richard Berman, the presiding judge, lifted the suspension and unnecessarily accused Roger Goodell of manipulating Brady's evidence.

McNally and Jastremski did not receive any punishment, but nobody seemed to mind, although Brady's punishment and the lack of punishment did have tongues wagging. He is a legend of the game, but controversies that he has been caught up in have tarnished his reputation somewhat.

Chapter 6

Cycling

Cycling has a long doping history that may very well stretch back to 1886, when Arthur Linton, a British cyclist, allegedly mixed up caffeine, cocaine, and a pesticide called strychnine in an effort to give him extra energy in a one-day race in Bordeaux. There are mixed accounts of the story, some claiming that he died from the concoction and others claiming that he lived until 1896, when his manager poisoned him. Either way, over the years to follow, many attempts would be made to cheat, many involving amphetamines. The first doping scandal that received widespread media coverage and cast a shadow over the sport involved Marco "the Pirate" Pantani.

Marco Pantani, the 1999 Giro D'Italia and Beyond

Pantani was known as "the Pirate" because of the bandana he wore, along with his thick earrings. His story is somewhat of a tragedy: a national Italian hero who went down as a doper without ever actually failing a doping test and who met an untimely death, shrouded in mystery, at only 34 years of age. The man drew a crowd of over twenty thousand mourners in his hometown of Cesenatico, where he was laid to rest. He was loved by Italians and by the world; he has been the subject of books and songs, as well as having been immortalized in several monuments and statues. Pantani drew a crowd like no other, but unfortunately, his career was much shorter than it could have been.

The Pirate is still widely regarded as the best climber that has ever lived. At the peak of his cycling career, he weighed just 57 kilograms (125 pounds), and when he cranked up the gears, jumped out of the saddle, and swung his bike from side to side, everything screamed athleticism. Pantani won the Tour de France and Giro d'Italia in 1998 and racked up sixteen individual stage wins across the two grand tours during his career.

It was in 1999 that performance-enhancing drug use allegations surfaced, and from that point on, Pantani was dogged by regular speculation. He was disqualified from the three-week-long Giro d'Italia after failing a hematocrit test. The medical test is used to measure red blood cell count; too low is a sign of anemia, and too high means an increased chance of blood clotting (Martin, 2022). However, in doping, the idea is to increase your red blood cell count, which means more oxygen, which in turn means increased muscle activity. Pantani's reading was more than 50% higher than the allowable level as set by the international governing body for world cycling. The measurement of red blood cell count via the hematocrit method is not a doping test. However, results that are much higher than what is permissible are a strong indication of doping. Even though Pantani was disqualified from the 1999 Giro, he had to wait until 2003 for a legal ruling. The court acquitted him because doping was not a criminal offense in 1999.

Back to 1999, and a particularly heinous article in the Italian newspaper La Repubblica. Accusations were leveled against Italian doctor Francesco Conconi, who had close ties with Doctor Michele Ferrari, who was later implicated in doping scandals involving Lance Armstrong. The newspaper claimed that Conconi had given a number of cyclists, including Pantani, doses of EPO between 1993 and 1998.

EPO is a subclass of substances called erythropoiesis-stimulating agents, which are used medically for kidney failure. In endurance sports such as cycling, EPO is used to increase red blood cell count, allowing for longer periods of high performance. The article in La Repubblica referred to a file found in a Biomedical Research Institute run by Conconi that contained information about the hematocrit levels of more than one athlete. Pantanis readings ranged between 40%–61% during the 1994 and 1995 seasons, according to records Conconi did not receive any criminal punishment, but word was that the presiding officer viewed the situation as morally wrong and a glorification of doping.

In 2002, Pantani was handed an eight-month ban by the Italian Cycling Federation for an insulin needle found in a hotel room in 2001. The pirate testified that the needle was planted and that he did not even stay in the room. On appeal, he was acquitted due to lack of evidence. The negative fanfare and the media circus had an effect on Pantani's mental health. He self-medicated with cocaine on and off before overdosing in a hotel room in

Rimini. The Italian public and the cycling fraternity were heartbroken, as a note found in Pantani's passport revealed how he really felt.

The Pirates manager read the note out at Pantani's funeral:

For four years I've been in every court; I just lost my desire to be like all the other sportsmen, but cycling has paid, and many youngsters have lost their faith in justice. All my colleagues have been humiliated, with TV cameras hidden in their hotel rooms to try and ruin families. How could you not hurt yourself after that? (CBS Sports, 2004)

Jan Ullrich Admissions

The German cycling phenomenon was probably born at the wrong time, given that he finished three Grand Tours of the Tour de France in second place behind Lance Armstrong. In any other era, he would probably have dominated the sport. There is reason to believe that during the 2000, 2001, and 2003 Tour de France races, Ullrich was not doping. Those were the years when he came in second place to self-confessed doper, Lance Armstrong. Ullrich, the Olympic gold medal winner in 2000, did admit to doping, but there was no evidence to suggest that he used any form of performance-enhancing drugs or tactics in 2000, 2001, or 2003.

Yes, he was a doper, but in the 2003 Tour de France, Ullrich displayed an admirable act of sportsmanship. Lance Armstrong and Ullrich were together, mid-climb, in stage 15, when Armstrong collided with a spectator, and Ullrich waited, which cost him a possible time advantage. Then, when Ullrich himself crashed in the final time trial, that earlier missed advantage and act of sportsmanship perhaps cost him the Tour victory. A gentleman and a doper, but at least one who owned up to his wrongdoing.

The Scandal

Jan Ullrich was set to start the 2006 Tour de France, in which he was touted as a favorite, along with Italian rider Ivan Basso. However, the two men would not even cross the start line on June 31. The day before, the German and Italian participants were suspended on claims of doping in the Giro d'Italia, which concluded on May 28. Ivan "the Terrible" Basso had claimed first place, while Ullrich had pulled out two stages before the conclusion of the event. The German cyclist went on to claim that retiring from the race was always the plan and that the doping allegations, which he denied, had nothing to do with it.

Before the Tour de France was even finished, Ullrich's T-Mobile team had sacked their star rider, via a communication to his lawyer. Anti-doping advocate and German biologist Werner Franke threw out completely speculative views that Ullrich had spent over €30,000 ($38,000) on doping products during a one-year period. In early August 2006, a German court granted an order preventing Franke from making any further public claims. Throughout the rest of 2006 and into early 2007, there was a lot of back and forth involving accusations, denials, and salacious media ongoings before Ullrich announced his retirement.

Ullrich was subject to further investigation by the International Olympic Committee, the German cycling authorities, and the Swiss Cycling Federation, none of which produced any adverse results. The Union Cycliste Internationale (UCI) launched an appeal with the Court of Arbitration for Sport, sitting in Switzerland, and in 2012, Ullrich was found guilty of doping when the appeal was upheld.

Despite all his prior denials, the German rider admitted to doping in 2013, but it wasn't a surprising announcement. One hopes that the cycling community, the German public, and the world don't forget that his three famous second places in the Tour de France were as a clean competitor.

The Lance Armstrong Doping Case

Cycling was traditionally a European-dominated and European-supported sport until a young American cycling hero came along in the late 1990s. His name was Lance Armstrong, and with his inspiring story as well as his seven-year dominance in the Tour de France, he popularized cycling world-wide. Unfortunately, he also exposed the level of doping in the world of grand tours. Doping was nothing new; it had been around in cycling for several decades, but the Armstrong scandal was on another level, and it prompted interest in the prior doping scandals, of which there have been many. once called the Tour de France, but never again.

The Racing History of Lance

Lance Armstrong was born Lance Gunderson to mom Linda and dad Eddie in 1971. Lance's folks got divorced when he was two, and within a year, his mother was married to Terry Armstrong. Linda Gunderson became Linda Armstrong, and Terry adopted Lance, who took his stepfather's name. Prior to his teens, Lance Armstrong had been running and swimming competitively. However, cycling beckoned at the age of 13, followed by triathlons, and at age 16 he turned pro. At age 18, Armstrong won the 1989 sprint-course triathlon nationals. He defended his title in 1990, after which he decided to drop swimming and running in order to focus solely on bike riding.

Team Motorola offered Armstrong a professional contract in 1992 after he finished second in the U.S. Olympic team time trial earlier in the year. He didn't fare well on the road, clocking a 14th-place finish. However, people started talking about Armstrong's promise as a rider when he won an individual stage in the 1993 Tour de France. He also won the coveted rainbow jersey in the 1993 World Championships, among several one-day classics and European stage races.

Over the next two seasons, the Motorola man won on a semi-regular basis, including a second stage victory in the 1995 Tour de France. The year after, Armstrong pulled out of the Tour de France, citing bronchitis, but managed to recover in time for the 1996 Atlanta Olympic Games. He finished sixth and twelfth respectively in the time trial and road race, by which time Armstrong was ranked seventh in the world of cycling, earning himself a lucrative offer from the French team Cofidis. Come October 1996, the young rider had started coughing up blood and feeling fatigued on a regular basis. He went for tests, which revealed that he had testicular cancer that had spread to the point where his body was riddled with it. So he traded his bike for a hospital bed and began treatment, even though his urologist was not confident that Armstrong had long to live.

Jump forward to February 1997 and a miraculous clean bill of health for Armstrong. Cofidis did not renew Armstrong's contract. However, the U.S. Postal Service team made him an offer, and he signed on the dotted line. It was October 1998; Armstrong threw himself into training and enjoyed the rewards the next year when he won the overall classification in the Tour de France. He won in 2000 as well, making it two in a row, and by 2005, Armstrong had notched up seven wins on the trot. The inspirational, hard-working, gritty American rider called it a day after his 2005 victory. However, he couldn't resist the pull of the sport and made a comeback in 2009, when he finished third in the Tour de France. The 2010 edition saw Armstrong claim 39th place before retiring in 2011, at the age of 39.

The Scandal Comes Out

Throughout his career, Armstrong was accused of doping on countless occasions. However, he never failed a test and constantly denied any involvement until January 2013, when he made the revelation live on air while being interviewed by Oprah Winfrey.

The Report

The United States Anti-Doping Agency (USADA), after a detailed investigation during 2011 and 2012, publicly alleged that Armstrong had trafficked drugs and engaged in doping. The allegations were based on a retroactive analysis of blood samples taken during Armstrong's last two professional seasons, 2009 and 2010. USADA laid official charges in October 2012 and called for Armstrong to be banned from competing in any World Anti-Doping Agency (WADA) sanctioned sporting events for the rest of his life. USADA succeeded, and Armstrong received the life ban in addition to being stripped of all cycling achievements from August 1998 until retirement. That meant that the seven-time Tour de France yellow jersey holder had to turn in all seven first-place finishes. There was speculation as to whether the riders who finished second over the consecutive winning periods would be declared winners. However, the final decision was that the second-place finishers would remain in their positions. In the meantime, every single one of Armstrong's sponsors, listed below, terminated their contracts with the disgraced bike rider:

- Anheuser Busch Brewers
- Nike
- Oakley
- Trek Bicycles
- FRS Energy Drinks
- Giro Helmets

- Honey Stinger Foods and Gels
- Radio Shack
- 24HR Fitness Health Clubs

The Legal Ramifications

Several civil lawsuits were brought against Armstrong. However, there was a criminal inquiry that overlapped the USADA investigations, beginning in 2010, with the end result of criminal charges being dropped in February 2012. Several of Lance Armstrong's former U.S. Postal teammates and other cycling insiders made statements implicating him in the doping scandal.

The Other Lawsuits

Floyd Landis, who rode for U.S. Postal between 2002 and 2004, was Armstrong's chief accuser. Landis called on the False Claims Act, which allows individuals to sue as representatives of the government on claims of fraud. The legal action was launched in 2010 and dragged on until 2018. A significant component was the production of emails sent by Landis, also an American rider, to team and individual sponsors. Other recipients included cycling officials, and the emails detailed Landis' continued use of performance-enhancing drugs. No names were left out, as Landis revealed that other cyclists and team members were heavily involved. One of those names was Lance Armstrong, whom Landis claimed had defrauded the U.S. government by receiving money from the U.S. Postal Service. The U.S. Department of Justice got involved in early 2013 for the purposes of reclaiming the alleged fraudulent amounts received by Armstrong and his crew. By April 2014, long after Armstrong's Oprah Winfrey confessions, Landis' lawyers had filed legal pleadings detailing statements that Armstrong had made under oath. The statements revealed that three doctors, including the highly controversial Michele Ferrari, as well as his trainer, Jose Marti, had supplied him with illegal drugs. Armstrong named the names of individuals that were tasked with transporting doping-related products and others that were in the know during the ongoing indiscretions. USADA banned Jose Marti and one of the doctors, Pedro Celaya, from cycling for eight years. Johan Bruyneel, a former Belgian professional cyclist and U.S. Postal team director, was given a ten-year ban for his continued involvement in the scandal.

The amount claimed by Floyd Landis on behalf of the U.S. Government from Armstrong under the False Claims Act was $100 million. The legal battle came to an end in 2018, with a settlement figure of $5 million, payable by Armstrong to the U.S. government. One could argue that Armstrong got off lightly, taking into account that U.S. Postal had paid Armstrong, and Johan Bruyneel's sports management company a total of $31 million between 2001 and 2004.

Where Is Lance Armstrong Now?

Lance Armstrong has endured public hatred, death threats, and social media promises to hurt his children and family. Being a cheat is disgraceful and embarrassing, but being killed for it or having your family harmed is a bridge too far. Armstrong has not shown much remorse and does not appear to have regrets, but maybe behind closed doors, out of the crosshairs of the media, he lets his demons out. Only he will know that, but I would venture to say that it is doubtful.

As of the time of this writing, Armstrong, now 51 years old, is still involved in the Livestrong Foundation despite resigning after his admissions of doping. He is a cancer warrior and helps countless patients and their families both financially and emotionally with the support of the foundation.

Armstrong owns a coffee shop and a bike shop in Austin, Texas. He is contracted to SRAM Corporation, where he provides technical advice to bicycle component manufacturers. He also has a stake in the Trek Bicycle Corporation and has started his own podcast called "*The Move.*" A particularly attractive facet of The Move is a five-day cycling holiday with Armstrong and some ex-pros and current cyclists in Mallorca, which is offered on an annual basis. So it seems those inside the cycling world may be more forgiving than many others, and despite his past sponsor withdrawals and fines, Armstrong is still a very wealthy man.

The one-time teenage sensation, cancer patient, and cycling phenomenon certainly leads a good life and still considers himself a seven-time Tour de France champion, as suggested by his tweets. Maybe he was the fall guy, and maybe cycling has become a clean sport, but one would not be remiss to have doubts about that.

The Floyd Landis Investigation

Although Landis was involved in the Armstrong saga, his doping exploits in the 2006 Tour de France had nothing to do with his then-retired, former teammate. Landis took the yellow jersey in the 2006 edition, but soon he would be answering some very difficult questions. Four days after stepping off the podium at the Tour de France, on July 27, 2006, it was announced that Landis' urine tests had identified unusually high levels of testosterone. Landis certainly came up with some unlikely, or at least unforeseen, excuses for his failed doping tests. Whiskey consumption was one reason; extreme dehydration was another; even gross errors in the testing process Landis rubbished the results of the test on sample A of his urine, done by the French government-appointed lab, but the testing of the B sample revealed the same results as the first. For some time, Landis was ridiculed, especially when he was stripped of his 2006 title. The United States Anti-Doping Agency (USADA) got to work, and an arbitration began on May 14, 2007. By the time it concluded on September 20 of the same year, Landis had been found guilty of doping, as expected. In December 2007, the French Anti-Doping Agency also came to a guilty conclusion, and Landis was banned from any and all competition in France for two years. Appeals followed, including an attempt to invalidate a decision made by the Court for Arbitration in Sport and the institution of federal litigation, with absolutely no success. Landis allegedly spent $2 million trying to clear his name and also wrote a book, "*Positively False*," in which he claimed that he was clean. All of the above fell by the wayside in 2010, when Landis made his admission of guilt. Everyone knew it already, but his book sales probably helped to mitigate his legal costs, and at least he can lay his head down at night with a clear conscience.

Is Cycling Clean Today?

If one goes by the times and the breaking of records set by dopers in the past, it would appear that the sport is still plagued by some sort of cheating. In the 2022 Tour de France, the general classification winner, Jonas Vingegaard, rode the fastest race in the 109-year history of the event. The previous holder of the record was that man Lance, so the cynics probably lean towards something nefarious. Climbing records were also smashed in the 2022 event, with the young American Brendon McNulty finishing the arduous Col d'Azet climb two and a half minutes faster than poor old Marco Pantani did it in 1997. The overall race pace was also alarmingly high, and reasons offered ranged from greater aerodynamic design quality to breakthroughs in nutrition and strong tailwinds, but questions will always be asked.

Then there is the question of Chris Froome, the tall Brit, and his magnificent victory on a grueling mountain stage in the 2018 Giro d'Italia. He battled plummeting temperatures for 80 kilometers (49 miles) on snow-lined roads to obliterate the competition during the nineteenth stage. Not everyone waiting for him at the finish line was a supporter. In fact, he finished with jeers and taunts brought on by a failed drug test the year before that, for all intents and purposes, went unrecognized. It was in the 2017 Vuelta de España when he violated the World Anti-Doping Agency's limit on the presence of a drug called salbutamol. The salbutamol entered his system via an asthma inhaler, and despite the tests revealing that Froome had twice the permissible amount of salbutamol, he denied that he had overused the inhaler. Technicalities abounded as Froome's team asserted that salbutamol is a controlled substance that is not on the banned list and that Froome's use of the inhaler did not amount to doping. The UCI has been pretty weak on the subject, and the matter has gone quiet in that sense. However, the detractors and the cycling-obsessed public have made it clear that Froome is worthy of a life ban. The question still remains, but it would seem that it will continue to go unanswered.

Creative Cycling Cheats

Doping is a pretty sophisticated business, with exact measurements, vein identification, needle concealment, urine test swapping, and carefully thought-out denials. However, there have been a host of cheating attempts that did not involve the same types of intricacies. The end results are always the same: the truth comes out, and the cheaters are revealed. There is more than one way to do it—several, it turns out.

The 1903 Tour de France

The world's most famous bike race got off to a cheating start in its very first edition in 1903. The culprit seems to have gotten away with it, but the circumstances were shady.

Hippolyte Aucouturier, the favorite to win the race, dropped out during the first stage between Paris and Lyon. The reason was that he was suffering from debilitating stomach cramps. Speculation was that Acouturier had combined wine and ether sniffing endeavors on top of undereating, which had undone the race favorite. The unproven conclusion was food poisoning, as claimed by Acouturier's team, and it seemed a logical explanation. Perhaps Aucouturier thought that a competitor purposefully tried to eliminate him from the race, so in 1904, it was his turn to hit back, and his team came up with an out-of-the-box way to ensure victory. They tied a fine piece of string to a cork, which Auconturier held in his mouth, while the other end of the string was attached to the team car. Had the roads been lined with spectators, as is the case with modern-day cycling events, the scenes would have been comical. The problem was that the driver went much faster than any bike rider could go, and when Auconturier finished only a few minutes after an official race vehicle, it became clear that there was foul play involved. Auconturier was disqualified, along with three other riders, amidst accusations of hopping onto a train to bypass a section of the route and engaging members of the public to block the roads with felled trees. The initial fifth-place finisher was shot up to the top of the podium as a result. His name was Henri Cornet, and the then-19-year-old remains the youngest ever Tour de France winner.

Gangs and Powder

Maurice Garin was a working-class hero of sorts who left chimney sweeping behind to become a cyclist. Reports state that he chain smoked and often had a cigarette hanging out of his mouth while laboring up hills on his bike. He certainly was not the healthy living type associated with participation in endurance sports, and after being asked how he won a 24-hour race in 1893, he credited it to his consumption of the following along the route:

- 19 liters of hot chocolate
- several containers of wine
- a coffee and champagne cocktail
- 5 liters of tapioca

- 7 liters of tea
- 2 kilograms of rice
- 45 cuts of chicken
- countless cigarettes

It was in the 1904 tour, the same race as the Cork Scandal, that Garin was nabbed for cheating. He was one of the men who boarded the train to skip part of the race, but that was not the only poker in the fire. Garin arranged for a gang of associates to put itching powder in the shorts of his competitors and to sprinkle broken glass and thumb tacks all over the roads to ensure that competitors would get punctures. Maybe Garin and his gang went too far and could have gone undetected, if they stuck to just the itchy powder. Like the cork incident in the same event, the itchy powder scenes must have been laughter-inducing.

Heavy Water

His nickname was "Kid Goat," and he was the first winner of the Tour de France after World War II. His real name was Jean Robic, and at 58 kilograms (127 pounds), the little Frenchman was built for hill climbing. Allegedly, in the 1947 race, his team would provide bottles of water containing mercury or lead at the top of the climbs. He would hang onto the bottles to take advantage of the increased weight on the downhills, then toss them aside for his team to pick up and hand them back to him at the top of the next climb. Robic was the pioneer of the scheme, but it didn't take long until many of the other riders were doing the same thing. As one can imagine, the secret couldn't be kept indefinitely, and the organizers of professional racers caught on and outlawed the illegal tactics.

Take a Right, No, Take a Left

In a race in Belgium during the 1950s, an English cycling sensation by the name of Pat Boyd didn't set out to cheat, but after having done so, found himself disqualified and very embarrassed. Boyd got a puncture, and the time it took to repair the tyre allowed the peloton to gain a significant amount of ground on the Englishman. He managed to catch up to a straggler, who told Boyd that he knew a shortcut through a back alley or two. When asked if he wanted to follow, Boyd agreed, and the straggler led him down an alternative route, allowing him to catch the peloton. The grateful Boyd finished inside the top ten, only to discover that his new friend had led him into the pack of riders from another race, which was happening simultaneously. Boyd was disqualified for failing to start the race and received a last place finishers card in the correct race. Probably one of the few occasions on which there was more hype about the loser than the winner.

Mechanical Doping

One could say that this is a step up from water bottles filled with lead and mercury. Yes, cyclists have attempted to cheat by fitting motors to their bicycles. Maybe it could be done in a social ride or a seniors event, but Femke Van den Driessche, a young Belgian woman, wasn't so lucky when she tried it in 2016. Driessche was competing in the Under-23 Cyclocross World Championships when, after her race, a bike inspection revealed a "not-so-secret" motor. Driessche was disqualified and banned for six years, but that still did not deter a competitor in an Italian Masters race. The 53-year-old, who was riding an Argon 18 bicycle, was pushing the 50 kilometer per hour (31 miles) mark in sections of the race that were not conducive to such speeds. The man didn't even win, but he lost his third-place medal after a heat scan detected a small motor device in his bike's seat tube.

Bike Switching

If you watch a grand tour or smaller stage race, you will see team cars all over the place with bikes on the racks as back-ups and swap-outs. But in 1963, bike swaps were only permitted upon mechanical failure. It was in the Tour de France that year when French rider Jacques Anquetil instructed a mechanic to cut his gear cable, allowing him to discard his original bike and grab a lighter one for the climb up the Col de la Forclaz as part of stage seventeen in that year's race. In 1963, Anquetil won the Tour de France, and the bike swap was seen more as a cheeky move than outright cheating. Anquetil won four Tour de France races in his career and, one could argue, made bike switching what it is today.

Chapter 7

Motorsport

At the mention of motorsport, the thought of extreme amounts of money pops into the heads of fans and non-fans alike. It costs about €2 million ($2,200,000) to rent a superbike per rider per season, and developing a high-level Formula One car, as of 2021, would have cost approximately $400 million dollars. With that kind of money flying around, just on bikes and cars, and the fervent desire to win, the history of motorsport has provided some scandalous sagas of large proportions.

The Great 2007 Formula One Espionage Controversy

Dubbed "Stepney-gate" due to Ferrari team member Nigel Stepney's involvement in the supply of confidential information to the McLaren team, The Englishman claimed that he was the victim of an elaborate conspiracy hatched by the powers that be at Ferrari, but many involved in the Formula One traveling circus remain unconvinced. Stepney was a mechanic of high acclaim who, quite ironically, died at age 56 in a motor vehicle accident in 2014. The circumstances were unclear, but it is certain that he was parked on a freeway. It would seem that Stepney dived out of his vehicle or jumped out from behind it so that he would be obliterated by a heavy goods vehicle. The driver of the heavy goods vehicle was an experienced trucker called Jan Byl, who couldn't do anything to avoid Stepney. There was wide speculation about suicide, but it was never proven. It is, however, plausible given Stepney's emotional trauma during and after the scandal.

The Whole Story

In 2007, McLaren's chief designer and a friend of Nigel Stepney convinced the Ferrari mechanic to provide information to McLaren prior to the start of the 2007 season. Stepney did so in the form of documents, amounting to nearly 800 pages of strictly confidential contents. Mike Coughlin, the chief designer, got his wife involved, and that's how he was busted. Mrs. Coughlin went to a local print shop to make copies of the documents so that the originals could be safely returned to Stepney. The owner of the shop had sight of what was being run through the copy machine and contacted Ferrari to convey his suspicions. Police subsequently raided Coughlin's home and discovered the incriminating material. Investigations found that McLaren had not been involved in any wrongdoing, but that decision was changed, and the team was fined €100 million ($147 million). They were also disqualified from the Constructors' Championship, which runs alongside the on-circuit racing. McLaren would have won the constructors' title that year, making the ban a seriously expensive punishment. The team always maintained that they were not disadvantaged in any way, which is debatable.

The plot ran deeper as Fernando Alonso, who was tied for second with Lewis Hamilton in the 2007 Drivers' Championship, started threatening to go public about his adverse treatment at McClaren. There was conjecture as to whether Alonso knew more about the espionage than what was in the public domain, but he grew tired of the whole thing and left McClaren with three years remaining in his contract. The FIA investigation found both Coughlin and Stepney guilty of industrial espionage, sabotage, and sporting fraud. Part of the verdict included information that incriminated Stepney for attempting to sabotage Kimi Raikkonen's car at the Monaco Grand Prix. Stepney was given a twenty-month prison sentence, which he never served, but he also never worked in Formula One again. Coughlin didn't get any jail time, but he did get banned from Formula One. He returned in 2011 as technical director for the Williams team, while Stepney made a comeback as a team director in the World Endurance Championship prior to his death in 2014. Another bit of irony is that Kimi Raikkon, of Ferrari, won the 2007 Drivers' Championship, meaning that the stolen information was nothing short of redundant. If Stepney's death was suicide, it could have been prevented if he hadn't gotten into the business of sabotage. Hindsight, however, is of no use, but something to consider is that neither Stepney nor Coughlin stood to benefit in any way unless there is unknown information waiting to be uncovered.

Crashgate

This scandal took place in 2008, shortly after Fernando Alonso left McClaren to join Renault. The French racing team was having a good season and improving as the races ticked by. The Singapore Grand Prix was earmarked for a Renault victory, and it was expected that Alonso would secure pole position. Unfortunately for Renault, Alonso was left high and dry on the track during qualifying as a result of a fuel issue. The Spaniard lined up 15th, a clear disadvantage, but he had a plan involving Nelson Piquet Jr. and the safety car. During lap 12, Alonso made a pit stop and rejoined the race at the back of the field. Piquet Jr. strategically crashed on turn seventeen, and the safety car was deployed. With the pit lanes closed, Alonso subtly jockeyed through the pack as the plan came to fruition, allowing him to take the win for his new team. Piquet Jr., the young Brazilian, had done his job, which included the risk of serious injury and being caught.

Renault had gotten away with it, and there must have been a huge sense of relief, except they hadn't gotten away with it. The Brazilian driver felt badly treated at Renault, and when he left the team in 2009, he alleged that he had been instructed to crash by team director Flavio Briatore, a man with a history of fraud stretching back to the 1980s. Pat Symonds, a British engineer, acted with Briatore, and with the might and power of his experienced seniors bearing down on him, Piquet Jr. was pressured into crashing as instructed. In exchange for his truthfulness, he was indemnified from the imposition of formal sanctions, but Symonds, after a confession, was banned for five years from working for any Formula One team. Not even six months later, Symonds' ban was overturned. Briatore was sentenced to life in prison, but this was quickly reversed. So, what is the purpose of punishment? Hardly a deterrent if it isn't even upheld.

Brakes, Weights, and Secret Tanks

In the early 1980's, there was an engine transition in Formula One cars from DFV engines to turbocharged engines. DFV is the acronym for "double four valve," and the Ford Cosworth DFV engine was launched in 1967. Obviously, improvements and modifications had been made over the years, but with turbocharged engines creeping into Formula One, the teams still using DFV engines, as per the Formula One Constructors' Association (FOCA), were at a power disadvantage. The solution was to reduce the weight of the cars in order to compensate for the power disparity.

How Did They Do It?

Some out-of-the box thinking led to the employment of water-cooled brakes, which had nothing to do with breaking. The minimum weight requirement in 1982 was 580 kilograms (1,278 pounds), and cars were weighed prior to the start of each race. To meet weight requirements, the vehicles would be outfitted with water tanks that served no purpose other than to add weight. Due to the positioning of the tanks, which were filled with water prior to the weigh-in, the water evaporated within a few laps, dropping the weight significantly. It was an ingenious plan, considering that prior to post-race weigh-ins, cooling fluids could be topped up. These endeavors did not violate regulations, but deception was the clear motive; there wasn't a large effort to keep it a secret.

Despite not breaking regulations but rather bending them significantly, Nelson Piquet (the father of Sebastian Piquet Jr.) and Keke Rosberg, who finished first and second, respectively, at the 1982 Brazilian Grand Prix, were disqualified. The inconsistency was that John Watson, the McLaren driver who initially finished fourth, was not disqualified, even though he used the same system as the winner and runner-up. It appeared that the thinking was that Watson's modification didn't help, which seemed nonsensical. Watson had done nothing differently than the first two racers, but he jumped from fourth to second, which was clearly unfair. The next round that season was the San Marino Grand Prix, and the enormity of the situation increased when it got political, causing most of the turbocharged engine teams to withdraw. FISA, the Federation Internationale du Sport Automobile, made a ruling that cars would be weighed after each race in the exact condition that they finished. The law was clear, the rules could not be bent, the dust settled, and Formula One racing continued. However, in 1984, a similar scheme was attempted but failed.

Tyrell and the Modified Water-Cooled Breaking Scheme

Like the 1982 scandal, Tyrell's use of water also had nothing to do with breaking. A water-injection system was used to spray water over inlet trumpets, which is said to improve power output and hence increase speed. Using a water-injection system wasn't actually illegal, but the Tyrell team used what are called "aromatics" to mix with water in the reserve tank during pit stops. The aromatics, such as lead and toluene, would increase the octane level in the fuel, which would boost performance; that was the illegal part. Because the little water and aromatics trick was an identifiable booster, it was considered an ancillary fuel source. After a brief investigation, Tyrell was suspended for the last three races of the 1984 season, and all previous results were expunged. It was a good try, but everything in terms of DSV versus turbocharged was put to bed in 1986, when Tyrell became the last team to ditch DSV in favor of the more powerful engine technology.

The San Marino Weight Cheat

By 2004, the British American Racing (BAR) team started producing the results expected of them since their formation in 1999. During the 2004 season, British driver Jenson Button had a number of top-three finishes, and his Japanese teammate, Takumo Sato, had designs on the Constructors' Championship. The 2005 season got off to a slow start, and by the time the San Marino Grand Prix arrived, BAR had not scored a single point. However, at Imola, Sato finished sixth and Button finished third on an overcast day in April 2005. This was a step in the right direction for BAR, but the team would not be around for much longer, as little did anyone know. The stewards did the usual post-race scrutinizing of the vehicles, and Button's car was found to be underweight. It was discovered that an extra fuel tank had been secretly installed and could hold about eleven kilograms of weight. The BAR team made claims that extra fuel was required to run Button's car and that all fuel was drained before scrutinization, in any case.

Initially, BAR's claims were accepted, but the International Court of Appeal, engaged by the FIA, found that BAR's assertions were untrue. Jenson Button was disqualified from the San Marino Grand Prix, as was Sato, even though the Japanese racer's car was above the weight limit. BAR was not allowed to compete in the next two races, Spain and Monaco, and was also handed a six-month suspended ban. Max Mosley, the president of the FIA, felt that the punishments were too lenient, but they were not changed, and by the start of the 2006 season, BAR was no longer in place. The racing team had been bought by Honda and was much in need of a facelift and some cleaner tactics.

The Nascar Cheats

NASCAR is an acronym for the National Associations for Stock Car Auto Racing, and is an internal 36 week long racing series in the United States. Compared to Formula One, NASCAR is a young sport, but its popularity is huge, having made great strides since the first race in Daytona Beach, Florida, in February 1948. It represents a part of Americana and has produced some definite legends over the years. Morgan Shepherd started his first NASCAR Cup Series race in 1970 and was still racing cars in 2015. Richard Petty won an astonishing total of 200 Cup Series races; Jeff Gordon became the youngest ever NASCAR champion at 24; and Dale Earnhardt, a seven-time champion himself, died on the track at age 49, prompting a series of safety improvements. The sport has evolved, as was expected, and the controversies have gone through their own evolution too.

Smokey Yunick

Henry Yunick would probably say that he was an innovator or a modifier, as opposed to a cheat. Since early childhood, Yunick has loved anything mechanical and built a working tractor when he was only 12 years old. He received the nickname "Smokey" from a track announcer while racing an Indian Scout motorcycle at age 15. The name stuck, but at that point, Yunick had no designs on racing cars. He joined the army as a young man and flew B-17 airplanes in Europe. When Yunick returned to the U.S., he opened a motor shop in Daytona Beach, Florida, where he met a stock car driver called Marshall Teague. Yunick started building engines for Teague, and it was obvious that the man had a talent when it came to anything mechanical. During his time, Yunick designed and built cars, managed teams, and raced, always with the intention of coming up with something more or better in order to make a vehicle travel faster.

Smokey's Fuel Line

During the 1968 NASCAR season, officials were puzzled about how Smokey Yunick's car had such a good fuel economy rate. There were suspicions that Yunick was using a tank larger than permitted, but an inspection revealed that the tank was of normal dimensions. However, the fuel line was almost three and a half meters long, with an inner diameter of eight and a half centimeters. The modification allowed the car to carry just over 20 liters of extra fuel, which is what made the economy rate appear so good.

The Secretly Bigger Tank

Yunick hatched another plan that would allow him to carry more fuel without failing a technical inspection. In order to conceal the difference in volume after installing a larger tank, Yunick would stuff a basketball inside it before the inspection. After the car was cleared, he would pop the basketball, allowing space for extra fuel and meaning less time spent in pit stops.

Cold Cold Fuel

Fuel contracts at colder temperatures, meaning that a tank can hold more fuel if the fuel is cold. Yunick kept his fuel just above freezing when filling up. After a few laps, the fuel would expand, allowing the car to get much better mileage than other cars on the track. It was a great idea, and one that could not be said to be illegal. However, NASCAR felt it necessary to impose a minimum temperature for race fuel.

The Exhaust Manifold

In the 1970s, one of Yunick's tricks was to get around a law that prohibited mechanics from drilling out exhaust headers on the manifold. With bigger passages comes greater speed, and Yunick achieved this by running an abrasive substance through the manifold. He was not using a drill, meaning that he was not breaking the law, just substantially bending it.

Jeremy Mayfield

The Kentucky born Jeremy Mayfield, has never been far from controversy. In April 2011, five of Mayfield's dogs were put down after an attack on a postal worker, and in November of the same year, methamphetamine was found in a safe on Mayfield's property. He was also found to be in possession of stolen equipment and machinery, believed to have belonged to businesses near his residence. Charges were brought, and Mayfield was lucky to get away without a felony. He pleaded guilty to two misdemeanors, i.e. possession of drug paraphernalia, and possession of stolen property. His relationship with NASCAR has been tumultuous over the years, especially concerning drug use allegations, and warnings of defamation lawsuits. In addition, Mayfield was embroiled in an illegal fuel debacle on 16 April 2000, while racing at Talladega SuperSpeedway. One would admit that Mayfield wasn't exactly the epitome of honesty, but in this case it is more than probable that he had nothing to do with what went on. Someone, likely a team member, mixed a fuel additive into Mayfield's fuel tank. The additive was used to increase the oxygen content in the fuel, which in turn increases the speed and performance of the vehicle. NASCAR came down hard on Mayfield, docking him 151 standings points, in addition to slapping the car owner, Michael Kranefuss, with a $50,000 fine. Peter Sospenszo, the crew chief was handed a suspension until 6 June 2000, and in response, Mayfield came out with a statement, containing the following: "I feel really bad for our fans and our sponsors. We hate what happened, but we have to keep moving forward." (Autosport, 2000).

In light of what had actually happened, Mayfield's apology was weak. Nonetheless, his team was caught and served their punishment, putting a lid on just another NASCAR scandal.

Denny Hamlin

Hamlin's obsession with speed began as a go-kart racer in Virginia State, before he was even ten years old. He stepped up to mini-stocks and debuted at Langley Speedway in a stock car event in 1998, at age fifteen. In 2004, Hamlin was racing in the NASCAR Craftsman Truck Series, and at the end of 2005, he had pocketed fifth place in the overall championship. In 2006, Hamlin claimed two season victories, and as his career progressed, his form was up and down from year to year, claiming 48 race wins, with his best result being runner-up in the NASCAR 2010 Championships. On July 27, 2014, however, Hamlin and his Joe Gibbs Racing (JGR) team attracted attention for all the wrong reasons. At the Brickyard 400 race in Indianapolis that year, Hamlin's third-place finish was revoked due to illegal modifications. The JGR team increased its aerodynamic ability by modifying the rear firewall of Hamlin's Toyota. The team felt harshly treated, as Hamlin lost 75 points and both his crew chief and car chief were suspended for 6 races, in addition to receiving hefty fines. The JGR team was intent on appealing the sanctions, asserting that nothing was done illegally, but decided against it, saying that they would move forward and not let the scandal impact future results. It was probably best for the JGR team to admit defeat and put it behind them, which is what seemed to be the case.

Ken Shrader

Missouri-born multiple-format racer Ken Shrader has experienced success in NASCAR's Cup Series, Xfinity Series, and Camping World Truck Series. Shrader, who debuted in 1981, has certainly amassed a fortune and is the co-owner of the Macon Speedway in Macon, Illinois. In mid-1993, Shrader was dragged into a controversy at a short course in Seattle, where he allegedly tampered with the engine system by adding a part that illegally increased performance. At the time, Shraders' car was owned by Hendrick Motorsports, and when the controversy broke, Hendrick's general manager, Jimmy Johnson, issued a statement saying that there was no intent to cheat. He added that the part had gotten onto the exhaust system by mistake and that he was unaware of it until after the race, as was Ken Howes, the team's crew chief. The argument put forward is that the engine was supplied by a vendor, who must have installed the part during manufacture and was ignorant of the illegality, like everyone else. The story seemed a bit far-fetched, and NASCAR imposed a four-race ban for Shroder, along with Joe Hendrick, founder of Hendrick Motorsports.

An appeal before the National Stock Car Commission was lodged. By this point it appeared that there was another illegal part, being in the manifold, which had been adjusted using a drill, in the same style as Smokey Yunick. If the appeal was unsuccessful, the four-race ban would stand, causing Shrader to lose out on $190,000. Ordinarily, the team would split the amount 50–50, so, more accurately, Shrader would be denied $95,000. Fortunately for the team, the suspension was lifted and fines were imposed instead. There is speculation as to the monetary value of the fines, but talk was that they were significant.

Shrader retired at the end of the 2013 season, but not completely, as he stayed involved in motorsport, winning NASCAR's Petty's Series in 2022 at the age of 67. At the time of this writing, the veteran racer currently lives in North Carolina, amid speculation that he will carry on competing in the 2023 season. The cheating scandal is now ancient history, and Shrader will be remembered as a legend of the sport.

Richard Petty

Nicknamed "the King," Richard Petty had no choice but to become a racing legend. His father, Lee Petty, competed in the first-ever stock car NASCAR season, and in time to come, he became a three-time NASCAR driver champion. The King started working in his father's pit at age 12, so by the time he was 15, he could do more than the adults. The Petty family saw Richard's cousin and brother inducted into the NASCAR Hall of Fame. His son also raced, and his grandson was tragically killed in a car accident during a practice session in New Hampshire. Richard has a history of victories, awards, inductions, and team ownership as long as his arm—and probably his leg too.

The King competed in 1,184 events throughout his career, including 27 wins in the 1967 season. No other driver has come anywhere close to the 27-point mark, and we may never see it surpassed. His iconic car color was dubbed "Petty Blue," as all four of his vehicles over the years were painted that color. His iconic number, 43, one above his father's number 42, found its way onto his Oldsmobile, Plymouth, Torino Cobra, STP Dodge, and Pontiac Grand Prix. He is also the subject of more than 5 books, and at age 82, there is no indication of slowing down. He doesn't race anymore but is still heavily involved in what could be dubbed "the Petty Family Racing World."

One may say that in a career as long as Petty's, along with the family history, there must have been one scandal along the way. It happened on October 9, 1983, at the Charlotte Motor Speedway, in North Carolina. Petty beat three fellow future Hall of Famers, Darrell Waltrip, Terry Labonte, and Benny Parsons, who were inducted in 2012, 2016, and 2017, respectively. After Petty's victory, his Pontiac was found to have left-side tires on the right side, which created a clear advantage due to the gradient of the track. His engine was also problematic; it was significantly over the cubic-inch limit, again creating a big advantage.

NASCAR officials soon got to work, as they met for several hours to decide on the most appropriate punishment. The ruling was a $35,000 fine and a deduction of 104 points. Petty's win was not revoked, which made no sense, although he released a statement saying that he knew nothing of the brazen cheating plan. He went on to tell the NASCAR world that his team was tired of losing to other teams that were cheating. This announcement certainly created speculation that Petty was aware of his team's shenanigans. There was no specification of what the other teams were doing in terms of Petty's assertions. However, NASCAR swiftly introduced a rule whereby a ban of three races or a twelve-week minimum ban would be issued if drivers modified cars as Petty and his team had done. Everyone quickly forgot, and Petty's die-hard fans maintained that the King was ignorant of the cheat, and one would suspect that Petty will stick to his story.

Mark Martin

Mark Martin, a quiet man from Arkansas who was groomed on dirt tracks, was a driver who never quite got there in NASCAR. He did have many second-tier number one spots, forty-nine to be exact, but in the big leagues, he was a perpetual second, third, and fourth place holder in the drivers' championship. Martin crossed the start line in NASCAR for the first time in 1981, and it took him six years to get his debut race win in 1987. Even though Martin didn't win much, he never seemed too concerned, or at least his demeanor indicated so. In 1989, he finished third in the drivers' championship, but there was an incident that he would rather have forgotten. It happened at the North Carolina Speedway in another second-place duel. The end result was a 25-point penalty, and the reason was that the left front springs on his Ford T-Bird did not meet the required number of coils. The crew chief, Ben Lesley, was slapped with a $5000 fine, and Jack Roush, the team, and car owner also lost out on 25 valuable points.

The very next season, Mark Martin lost the series to Dale Earnhardt, but if one speculates, the Roush Racing speedster probably would have won had he not attempted to cheat again. That 1990 race in question was on the asphalt at Richmond International Raceway, where the Roush team fitted an impermissible carburetor on Martin's famous number six Ford. His punishment was a docking of 46 points, and come the season's end, he finished 26 points behind Earnhardt. There were another two scandalous incidents, one of which saw Ben Leslie receive a fine ten times the size of his coil-gate penalty. In this case, Martin's car was set too low, which was revealed in the post-race inspection.

Many are of the opinion that Martin was the best driver that will never be remembered because he couldn't quite crack the big leagues. However, that may be a good thing for the mild mannered Arkansas man, seeing he proved to be a cheat; a forgotten cheat perhaps.

Carl Long

Although Carl Long was a relative latecomer to NASCAR, he began racing track and stock cars in his mid-teens. He won the former in 1987, on the South Boston Speedway, and the latter in 1990, in Orange County. Long began NASCAR racing in the late 1990s, and the sport that he so diligently served for 10 years after his debut race celebrated that 10-year anniversary with some very harsh treatment. According to some fans and fellow drivers, NASCAR turned the whole situation into a farce.

Long was fined $200,000 after his engine was discovered to be slightly larger than required. It probably wouldn't have been discovered if the engine hadn't malfunctioned during practice for the NASCAR Sprint Series Cup event that ran in North Carolina. The main race was on May 18, 2009, but Long would not cross the start line. Being "caught" at practice on May 15, 2009, was enough to convince the NASCAR bigwigs to not only fine Long an outrageous amount but also to penalize him 200 driver points. Long and his wife DeeDee also lost 200 owner points as co-owners of the car. On top of all of that, Long was served with a 12-race suspension, the longest in NASCAR history at the time.

Long, whose team can only be said to be low-budget, made an appeal to the NASCAR commissioner, relying partially on the fact that he could not pay the fine. The only aspect that was reduced was Long's suspension, to eight weeks. The really sad part is that Long had purchased the engine from a man who had been building them for many years. Ernie Elliot was his name, and despite Long explaining that Elliot had told him that everything was in order with the machine, the fine still remained. Poor old Carl Long really did get dealt a crushing blow. He is probably one of the few motorsport drivers involved in a controversy, so sympathy is due.

The Lesson

The lesson is a hard one to be very specific about. Don't cheat is the obvious answer, but one can't help but be frustrated by the complete inconsistency of the various controlling bodies. In any form of hearing, inquiry, or investigation, all one can ask for is consistency of outcome.

Chapter 8

Boxing

One could say that boxing has been around as long as humankind has been around. It is the way to settle a feud or win an argument. However, in regulated circumstances, it is a sport of fitness, skill, athleticism, and money. The first evidence of boxing as a sport dates back to 3500 years, as evidenced by images created by the Minoans, a society in what is now known as Crete. It was the Greeks who popularized boxing as a sport, and fights were usually for honor and pride. However, it would appear that certain encounters garnered prizes, most often cattle. The loser was the first to pass out, be knocked out, tap out, or die. There were no rounds, and anything from eye gouging to headbutting was allowed. As time went by, the death toll started to rise considerably, until an intervention by boxer Jack Broughton took place in 1743. The Englishman instituted new rules, prohibiting certain methods of attack and emphasizing the thirty-second count out. Of course, the world was a bigger place, and due to relatively minimal travel, other sets of rules developed in other countries. Bare-knuckle fighting was the order of the day in the mid-1700s, but by the late 1800s, gloves started to enjoy wide use. However, as the early twentieth century arrived, boxing became a sport of the minority and was even banned in some countries. The solution was for fights to be held in illegal gambling halls, hidden from the authorities. Boxing and gambling have long had a symbiotic relationship that has made some but destroyed many.

Irish immigrants became a dominant force on the American fighting scene and were at the top of their collective infamy by 1915. It would take another fourteen years until black men were allowed to box in officially sanctioned events. The year was 1929, but the black community had to wait until 1937 for its first Heavyweight Champion of the World, Joe

Louis. American dominance, especially among black boxers, has ruled ever since, and no less than 431 world champions have been from the United States as of January 2023.

From violence in the ring to recreational drugs at the parties to performance-enhancing drugs in the gym, boxing certainly does not have a clean reputation. Many scandals have received widespread media coverage, elevating competitors to legendary status for all the wrong reasons. In many cases, boxing fanatics love a big blowout or a sensational press story, but even when the truth is revealed, the die-hards, and there are a lot of them, will never waiver in their support of the bad boys.

The Bite Fight

No boxing fan from the 1990s will ever forget the rematch of the World Boxing Association (WBA) Heavyweight Championship on June 28, 1997. Mike Tyson took on Evander Holyfield in the bout, and the world saw something animalistic. In his 17-year career, Holyfield participated in 57 fights, taking home 44 victories, including 29 knockouts. Some good numbers without a donut, but Tyson had a much more prolific career, losing only six professional fights. He retired with 50 wins under his belt, 44 of which were knockouts, but he did bite part of a man's ear off. That man was Evander Holyfield, and as the world watched in disbelief, they probably never expected Tyson to be stripped of his boxing license. A huge fine, yes. A disqualification, yes. A substantial ban, yes. However, was having his license taken away too much? Well, it depends on who you ask, but whatever anyone says, the act remains deplorable. Holyfield and Tyson had a great rivalry, going back to the 1984 Los Angeles Olympic qualifier. Tyson lost, and Holyfield headed to the Games, but he didn't get past the semi-final, where he faced Kiwi fighter Kevin Barry. It wasn't so much that Barry won as it was that Holyfield was disqualified. Allegedly, the American boxer had punched Barry despite the referee having signaled a break. It seemed a marginal call, but an appeal did not save Holyfield. He managed to pick up the bronze, and three months later, he became a full professional, in November 1984. Tyson, without having been to the Olympics, thought it best to turn pro in 1985. The two men had very rapidly gone from potential amateur teammates to professional rivals, and maybe that all came to a crescendo.

The fight took place in Nevada and was hosted by the MGM Grand in Las Vegas. 139 seconds into the first round, a powerful right from Holyfield sent shockwaves through

Tyson's body. He pushed back and avoided danger before the bell. The second round saw Tyson on the receiving end of a Holyfield headbutt as he dipped below a wild punch. Head-butting had been a contentious point in the first fight, with Tyson claiming repeatedly that Holyfield was doing it intentionally. As far as officials were concerned, replays exonerated Holyfield, as the decision was that there was no intention. Tyson recovered; a cut above his right eye became noticeable, and one can imagine that he was about to be pushed over the edge of anger. His rage was visible in the third round, and even though he came out at first without his mouthguard, his second entry from his corner produced an all-out attack on Holyfield. With about 40 seconds remaining in the 3rd round Holyfield managed to get his arms around Tyson to hold him in a clinch. Tyson was having none of it, as he managed to roll his head into a position where he could bite down as hard as he could on his opponent's right ear. In no time, an inch of Holyfield's bleeding ear was on the canvas after being spat out by Tyson. It must have been a seriously painful injury, as displayed by Holyfield, and as the referee called a time-out, Tyson shoved his competitor in the back. Mills Lane, the man in charge of the bout, immediately sent Tyson to the neutral corner in an effort to regain some form of calm. Holyfield still wanted to continue, which meant that Lane had some thinking to do. The ringside doctor gave the go-ahead for Holyfield to carry on, so Lane docked Tyson two points. Maybe it wasn't a great idea, considering that Tyson, who claimed that his opponent's completely detached ear was the result of a punch, had a go at Holyfield's left eye after the fight resumed. The left ear was severely bitten but not severed at all. However, Lane did what he should have done after the first bite and disqualified Tyson, meaning that Holyfield maintained his status as WBA Heavyweight Champion of the World.

After the Disqualification

Security converged on Holyfield's corner in order to protect him from a rampaging Tyson, who was escorted back to his corner by security. Through the microphone, Lane addressed everyone present and stated that his experience had led him to believe that the bites were, well, bites; completely intentional. When interviewed by the press, Holyfield had a not-so-subtle dig at Tyson, saying that his fiery opponent would rather have been disqualified than knocked out. Tyson, on the other hand, was talking to the press as he walked to the locker rooms when a fan threw a bottle of water at him—a Holyfield fan, one would imagine. Tyson and two men from his crew climbed up into the stands while showing the crowd the middle finger and other obscene signs. Before anything violent ensued, the men were held back and led away. Holyfield quickly forgave Tyson, not that the latter apologized, but rather he maintained that the bites were payback for the headbutts. Ultimately, Tyson was fined $3 million, not enough to dent his bank account but definitely enough to annoy him intensely.

The Reunion

Tyson's career and post-career have been tainted by controversy, including a guilty conviction for rape, for which he served a touch under three years. The boxer, known as the "Meanest Man in the World," got himself into some drug-related trouble and was involved in an innocuous scuffle or two.

However, as is often the case, he got himself together as he grew older and learned from his life events. Holyfield didn't attract quite as much scandalous attention as Tyson over the years. However, he found himself in financial trouble and had marital issues and child maintenance problems.

Despite having made mistakes and done things that they probably shouldn't have done, they both took advantage of their privileged positions to do a lot of good. Holyfield created a foundation that supports programs for economically disadvantaged children, and Tyson has been heavily involved in charity work. The two former heavyweights have put the bite fight so far behind them that neither man probably ever thinks of the 1997 bout that shook the boxing world. Of course it was wrong, but the ability of the men to bury the hatchet is a testament to the beauty of sport and humanity.

Forgiveness

Should he be forgiven? Well, Holyfield did. All one can conclude is that Mike Tyson is probably a deeply emotionally troubled man, but he will always be one of the best heavyweights that the world has ever seen. In light thereof, as well as the time that has passed, yes, he should be forgiven.

Antonio Margarito's Tampered Gloves

The orthodox stance, at 1.8 meters tall, was how Antonia Margarito and his older brother learned to box in a local Tijuana gym. Margarito Junior, known mostly as Tony, garnered the nickname "El Tornado de Tijuana," meaning "The Tijuana Tornado." He turned pro in 1994 at age 15, winning his first 5 fights in a row. He was 16 by the time he lost for the first time as a paid fighter and would go on to lose only 7 more throughout his career. He finished off with three wins on the trot over Jorge Paez Junior, Ramon Alvarez, and Carson Jones, respectively. The Tijuana Tornado's record cannot be disputed as being sterling. He defended his welterweight world championship no less than seven times, and when he hung up his gloves, Margarito had fought in 50 bouts, lost 8, and knocked out opponents in 27. There was that one niggly fight, however, in which he broke the rules, and dangerously so.

What Happened?

Shane Mosley and Antonia Margarito were scheduled to square off at Los Angeles' famed Staples Center. The fight was on January 24, 2009, but before it even started, Mosley's trainer, Naazim Richardson, demanded that the Tijuana Tornado's gloves be inspected. Inspectors found that Margarito indeed had illegal wraps, which they unceremoniously confiscated. Margarito had tried to cheat, but his efforts were thwarted early enough for one to say that he really didn't cheat. The fight went ahead, and Margarito took a pounding, losing by knockout in the ninth.

It was later discovered that the plan was for the wraps to harden as the fight went on. To achieve that, Margarito's trainer, Javier Capetillo, pasted a substance under the wraps. It wasn't exactly plaster of Paris, but something similar that hardened as it mixed with Margarito's sweat.

The Punishment

Both the boxer and trainer were banned for twelve months. Capitello claimed that it was an innocent mistake that he had made and that Margarito only found out about the substance upon inspection. Maybe the latter is true, but it is a very strange mistake to make, leaving a lot of conjecture as to the truth of the former part of Capitello's story.

Margarito then came out and said that he knew all along and that it was most certainly not a mistake. 12 months is not a long time when one considers the damage that can be done with a hardened substance in a boxer's glove. The men got off very lightly and provided the media with ammunition to castigate them. Of course, getting caught is never the intention, but the fallout should have been expected in the case of being busted.

Sugar Shane Mosley

Yes, it is the same Shane Mosley who was nearly crushed by Antonia Margarito's plaster of Paris gloves. We have to go back to 2003 in order to explore the time when Mosley was on the other side of a scandal. The man nicknamed "Sugar" was definitely a great fighter, and his record is clear evidence of that. He was a three-weight-class world champion, which is some feat, and he also had a penchant for knockout victories in title fights, having racked up twelve in his professional career. Mosley remained undefeated in the first 38 fights of his career. The Boxing Writers Association crowned him fighter of the year in 1998, as did the International Boxing Hall of Fame in 2000. Sugar Shane was only knocked out once in his career, and he also only used EPO once. One may be fact and the other fiction, but who knows? They might both be facts.

Just like in cycling, injecting extra EPO raises the red blood cell count, allowing more oxygen to flow to the muscles and thus facilitating longer endurance performance thresholds. Victor Conte was the man who explained all of this in detail to Mosley, and he certainly knew his stuff. Conte founded the Bay Area Laboratory Co-Operative, which is best known for producing the USADA-banned performance-enhancing drug tetrahydrogestrinone.

Conte has a habit of making enemies, and while Mosley was an acquaintance at best, it is safe to say that the two men do not like each other. To Mosley's credit, he openly admitted to using steroids and EPO; however, in his next sentence, he immediately discredited himself by claiming that he did not know that they were illegal.

Mosley's use of EPO took place during the build-up to his light-middleweight match with Oscar de la Hoya. During questioning under oath, Mosley was shown a calendar detailing instructions as to what to inject, when to inject it, and what the cost of the supply was. Surprisingly, Sugar Shane was never banned because he never tested positive for a banned substance, despite admitting to using steroids and EPO.

Conte became very vocal about the scandal, vociferously insisting that Mosley was completely aware of the illegality of the injecting saga. In this sense, Conte was being honest, and although a much-respected figure, he admitted to money laundering and an illegal conspiracy to distribute steroids in 2005. These admissions landed Conte in jail, but there were more legal battles to come. In 2008, Mosley filed a defamation suit against Conte. His lawyers must have been rubbing their hands in glee, safe in the knowledge that Conte had spoken the truth, to which Mosley had admitted. The lawyers knew they wouldn't win, but there was money to be made. The suit dragged on for over two years, amid media speculation, slanderous reporting, and even YouTube coverage, whether people were interested or not. The matter was dismissed in 2010, leaving Mosley bitter and angry, with Conte probably not giving it another thought.

Conte has also been involved in doping scandals involving professional track athletes Marion Jones and Dwain Chambers, as well as alleged baseball doper Barry Bonds. Conte also has a beef with MMA founder Dana White and is clearly a bad cheating influence. That is not to say that the unpunished Sugar Shane Mosley should not be held morally accountable.

The Mob and the Raging Bull

Initially dubbed the "Bronx Bull," the Italian-American middleweight and light heavyweight fighter, Jake LaMotta, had a career that saw him compete in over one hundred professional bouts. He was also known as "the Raging Bull" and was a man to be feared, especially given his associations with the mob. He didn't really have much choice, just like when he was a boy, and his father made money by pitting his son against other youngsters, bare-knuckled. Spectators would throw coins down, and LaMotta senior would collect them as fast as possible. The Raging Bull refined his skills at reform school after a failed robbery, and in 1941, at the age of 19, he turned professional. In the ring, he had an uncanny ability to ride and roll with punches, remaining standing when many other fighters would have gone down. For this, he became known as "the man with the best chin in boxing."

The $20,000 Fix

LaMotta was without a doubt the favorite to beat Billy Fox in 1947, but the mob had offered LaMotta the handsome sum of $20,000 to throw the fight. The betting ring run by the mob put their plan into action a few hours before the fight by throwing down a plethora of bets on Fox, and LaMotta knew what he had to do. The Raging Bull faked a knockout to collect the money, but that was just a sweetening of the deal. The mob got what they wanted, made some decent loot on the fight, and LaMotta got what he really wanted: a shot at the middleweight champion, Marcel Cerdon. In those days, the mob essentially ran boxing, and if LaMotta had his heart set on taking on Cerdon, he had to comply. One could argue that his intentions were not nefarious but rather a case of choosing the lesser of two evils.

13 years after the fixed bout, LaMotta appeared before a brash Tennessee State Senator with a cross to bear against organized crime in boxing. Estes Kefauver, the senator and head of the State Senate Subcommittee on Antitrust and Monopoly in Professional Boxing, was the man asking the questions, and LaMotta was not there to lie. Also present were another senator, Philip Hart, and a disingenuous-looking lawyer by the name of John G. Bonomi. LaMotta answered the questions honestly and confirmed what was already known. He stuck by his justification for losing to Fox, and in any case, he still wore the pride of victory against Marcel Cerdon.

LaMotta didn't have an easy life, although much was his own doing. The Raging Bull was married seven times and got into some hot water while running a nightclub. He allegedly introduced an underage girl to an associate for sexual behavior.

LaMotta released his personal memoirs under the title "*The Raging Bull: My Story*" in 1970, and a decade later Martin Scorsese directed a film by the same name. LaMotta was only ever going to be played by one actor, Robert DeNiro. The film garnered a lot of attention, and both the director and lead actor received critical acclaim.

All in all, one could say that LaMotta was a troubled man, but a man who certainly clung onto life until he passed away at the age of 95, still maintaining legendary cult status.

Luis Resto's Tampered Gloves

Before the age of 15, Luis Resto was a resident at a facility for the mentally disturbed as a result of an assault on one of his teachers. With the benefit of hindsight, that incident was probably an early indicator of the type of man he would become—nothing more than a violent criminal. Resto turned pro in early 1977 and got off to a good start, with seven wins on the trot, before finding himself passed out on the canvas at the hands of opponent Bruce Curry during their March 1978 bout. Resto was not largely successful or known outside of the New York scene for several years, but he changed all of that when he went into the ring on June 16, 1983, knowing that within his gloves lay the ability to kill his opponent. It was a decent undercard fight at best, and Resto's opponent, Billy Ray Collins, took a pounding for ten rounds at Madison Square Garden. Collins was the favorite and never looked like giving up; he got in a good few punches, but by the end of the fight, he could hardly see out of his shrunken, blood-red eyes. The rest of his face was swollen and looked like it was about to burst. After the fight, Resto congratulated his opponent and ended up shaking Collins' father's hands with his gloves still on. The father, also named Billy, thought that Resto's gloves felt odd and called for an official inspection, which revealed that the gloves had been doctored. Panama Lewis, Resto's trainer, had removed padding from his charges' gloves, and although Resto denied any knowledge at the time, he later revealed that he was fully aware and also knew of the plaster that Lewis had applied to his handwraps.

The immediate fallout was a one-year suspension of Resto's boxing license, but it took almost three years until legal sanctions were imposed. In 1986, Resto and his trainer, Lewis, were found guilty of conspiracy, possession of a weapon, and assault. Of course, the "weapon" was the glove and strapping combination. Considering Collins' eye was so badly damaged that he was ruled out of boxing forever, the jail sentences of two and a half years for the fighter and one year for the trainer seemed very light. Collins was terribly affected by his career being cut short so suddenly. He dove into depression and self-medicated with alcohol, which was ultimately his undoing, as he crashed his car while under the influence, leading to his death. Speculation abounded, with many citing Resto as the catalyst and, further, that the crash was a suicide, planned by Collins in advance.

Resto was 28 at the time of the fight and maintained denials of any knowledge of glove tampering until he appeared in an Eric Drath documentary in 2009. The flick was called "Assault in the Ring," and it shows the broken side of Resto as he speaks of his ongoing guilt. The once-violent teen has applied countless times over the years for the reinstatement of his license and for the granting of a license allowing him to become a second as part of a fighters' team. Resto wrote the test for the latter in 2011, which he passed, but the New York State Athletic Commission would not grant the license based on the fact that, if granted, Resto would find himself in a position to do the same thing that he and Lewis had done in 1983. As of the time of this writing, Resto still does not have a license and has faded into something of a nobody, training kids in Bronx gyms. The man will probably carry the regret with him as long as he lives.

IBF Founder Bribery

In the mid-to-late 19th century, a magazine named the Police Gazette, which had nothing to do with cops, was a New York-based sporting magazine. It gained popularity in the early 1900s, and world champions were officially listed in the Gazette before they could be considered legitimate champions. Aside from that, the sports publication was merely a publication and not a sanctioning body in boxing. As 1920 became 1921, the term "title fights" enjoyed more mainstream use and became officially sanctioned under the newly formed National Boxing Association. As time went by, other bodies were developed, and as of 2010, to be classified as the undisputed champion of the world, a boxer would have to be registered with and recognized by four bodies:

1. The World Boxing Association (formerly the National Boxing Association)

2. The World Boxing Council

3. The International Boxing Federation

4. The World Boxing Organization

The third body, the International Boxing Federation (IBF), is of particular interest due to its association with its founder and alleged criminal, Robert W. Lee. In 1983,

Lee applied for a position as president of the World Boxing Association (WBA). He was unsuccessful, so he got together with some colleagues to form the IBF. During his time, Lee faced 33 felony charges, and his son, who joined Lee as part of the IBF, was charged with nine felonies. Among the father and son team, the charges ranged from tax evasion to racketeering, money laundering, and interstate travel in aid of racketeering. When the story broke, boxing promoters were outspokenly forthcoming as to information stating that payoffs were endemic within the IBF ranks.

The FBI and several federal prosecutors entered into a comprehensive investigation that uncovered frowned-upon behavior that appeared illegal. After four years, the matter made it to trial, and some of the promoters, namely Cedric Kushner and Bob Arum, gave testimonies confirming their assertions that payoffs were a regular occurrence. The trial was protracted, as 80 audiotape recordings, consisting of hours upon hours of discussions about tampering with rankings, were played to the jury. The recordings came about through C. Douglas Beavers, head of the IBF ratings committee. Beavers was granted immunity from prosecution due to his role as an informant. The allegations named Lee and other officials as recipients of approximately $338,000 from promoters and managers for various favors. The judge revoked Lee's authority to operate within the IBF and ordered that a new president be appointed. Furthermore, the sanctioned body was assigned a court official to monitor operations.

The recordings revealed that Dino Duva, of a promotions company called "Main Events," paid Lee off to schedule a title fight for junior middleweight Fernando Vargas. The boxer remains champion, but the promoter left Main Events. The scandal had a much wider reach, involving Bob Arum, a former George Foreman promoter who "gifted" $100,000 to the IBF in exchange for a fight between Vargas and an unranked German fighter named Axel Schultz.

Surprisingly, Robert W. Lee was only found guilty on six of the 33 charges and was sentenced to 22 months in prison and given a fine of $25,000. The decision was definitely not rushed, considering that the jury deliberated for a total of 15 days. Lee Jr. got off on all nine charges, and not one of the boxers showed any guilt whatsoever. The public was left wondering how many more bribes exchanged hands, because it surely could not have only been the few that were revealed.

Chapter 9

A Sundry of Cheating Scandals

Athletics, swimming, and even Australian Rules Football have all had their share of scandals. It wouldn't be remiss to assume that every sport has had some sort of cheating attempt, and this chapter looks at the best of the rest when it comes to abuse of the rules.

The Dirtiest Race in History

Canada has not been known to produce many world-class Canadian-born track athletes. However, in recent times, 100- and 200-meter star Andre De Grasse, born in Ontario to a Trinidad and Tobago-raised mother and a Barbadian father, has most certainly become world-class. At the time of this writing, the Sprint King, as he is known in Canada, is a 6-time Olympic Champion and national 200-meter world record holder. De Grasse's 1990s contemporary is Jamaican-born Donovan Bailey, who moved to Canada at age 14. Bailey holds the Canadian national 100-meter record and is a former Olympic Gold Medal winner. The year was 1996, and the venue was Atlanta, the host city of the Games. Not only did Bailey cross the tape first, but he broke the world record. He hung on to the title of "fastest man in history" until 1999, when the Kansas Cannonball, Maurice Green, dipped under the mark set by Bailey.

Another legend in the shortest track race is also Jamaican-born, and like Donovan Bailey, he moved to Canada in his early teens. He goes by the name of Ben Johnson and became a national hero when he won the 100-meter dash at the Seoul Olympics in 1988. That moniker did not last long but was replaced by the tag of national embarrassment, as a few days later the sprinter tested positive for a steroid called stanozolol. There were strong suggestions that five of the other competitors had also doped, leaving only two clean sprinters. For this reason, the Seoul 100-meter was dubbed "the dirtiest race in history," but the only athlete that faced repercussions was Johnson.

The Alleged Cover Up

At first, the claims seem outrageous, but upon further thought, Dr. Wade Exum's theory is that international 100-meter racing was subject to a 12-year doping cover-up. Over 100 sprinters, 19 of whom had won Olympic medals, were allegedly involved in the racket, in which Carl Lewis may or may not have participated. Lewis, who was not only a sprinter but also a long jumper and perhaps the best in athletics history, won the 1988 Seoul race after Ben Johnson's disqualification. Earlier that year, Lewis had a 12-week ban for doping overturned by the U.S. Olympic Committee, allowing him to compete in Seoul. One must not forget that sprinters have been known to take performance-enhancing drugs and steroids, allowing them to train harder and longer in the build-up to major events. The idea is to time the use of the aforesaid so that traces are out of the system just before the event. A good tactic, but one that is risky, made worse by random drug tests; a risk worth taking.

The media cried politics; the 200 and 400-meter gold medalists in Seoul were two Americans, who had also tested positive in the U.S. Trials, along with Lewis. In simple terms, America wanted glory and had to quickly snub accusations as they tried semi-successfully to sweep the Lewis fiasco under the carpet. At a later stage, it was discovered that Floyd Heard and Joe DeLoach tested positive for three illegal stimulants; who were they? Carl Lewis' training partners.

The Sanction

While the American athletes got off scot-free, Ben Johnson served out a two-year suspension, after which he attempted to return to athletics. The Canadian speedster put in an average performance at the 1992 Olympic Games and shortly thereafter received a lifetime ban for doping. He admitted to doping as early as 1981, but managed to keep all titles and records during his self-avowed years of performance-enhancing drug use. Johnson was unfortunate; he was disqualified for the same thing as Lewis, just a few months after Lewis' pre-Seoul Olympics ban was lifted. One was kept quiet, the other was publicized, and the lack of fairness in sanctions due to cover-ups was highlighted.

Rosie Ruiz Fakes Boston Marathon Win

It was eight years after women were given permission to compete in the Boston Marathon that Rosie Ruiz decided to run only part of the race. The 28-year-old athlete entered the Boston Marathon by submitting her 1979 New York City Marathon time in order to qualify. Her Boston Marathon victory on April 21, 1980, blew her qualifying race time out of the water by 26 minutes, immediately raising eyebrows. Other guilt-inducing factors were present, including her lower body physique, which was not muscular enough to belong to an elite long distance athlete. An absolute giveaway was that nobody saw her, except for two young college students, according to whom Ruiz not so subtly appeared out of a crowd of spectators, just 800 meters from the finish line. The long list of those who did not see her on the route included photographers, spotters, spectators, and the actual leaders. Jacqueline Gareau was the confirmed number one placeholder, about thirty kilometers into the marathon, but no other woman passed her, making Ruiz's win completely impossible.

Ruiz was rightly disqualified, then involved herself in criminal activity, which she was equally bad at hiding as she was at cheating in sports. She went to trial in 1982, where she received a five-year probation term for siphoning $60,000 from an employer. A year later, Ruiz got three years of probation, this time for being part of a cocaine deal. Is it easier to cover up fraud and drug dealing, race-cutting, or none of them? Ruiz, who died of cancer in July 2019, cannot tell us, but one would conclude that she was pretty unskilled at all three.

A Few Golf Scandals

Golf is an up-and-down game; it is not possible to be outstanding every weekend. To fix a tournament in a way that a golfer finishes in a second position is one tick left of impossible, and if it happened, it would be astounding. There are, of course, other ways to cheat.

Phil Mickelson's Gambling Misdeeds

To golf fans, Mickelson is one of the most liked golfers on the PGA Tour, due to his friendly demeanor and light-hearted exchanges with the crowd. Also known as "Lefty" for obvious reasons. Mickelson, without a doubt, has the best flop shot in the game and is often seen rescuing himself from adverse situations with shots that defy logic. The rest of his game is pretty good too, as evidenced by over 40 outright tournament wins, including the Open Championship, the PGA Championship twice, and the U.S. Masters on three occasions. As one can imagine, Mickelson is hardly short of money, but it is well known that he has lost ridiculous amounts of cash through gambling. Like alcoholism or drug dependency, gambling is a legitimate addiction, and Mickelson has on several occasions acknowledged that. His biography, written by Alan Shipnuck, contains details of ongoing therapy to suppress the addiction. Mickelson himself described it as "reckless and embarrassing," as well as having estimated losses of over $40 million over a four-year period, between 2010 and 2014. To most people, that figure is huge, but taking into account a three-year, $277 million deal to play on the LIV tour, signed in 2022, Mickelson will never go short. Despite Mickelson's embarrassment, none of his gambling gambits were illegal, but there was an ugly incident in the world of insider trading.

What Happened?

Lefty was friends with a former small-time hustler and betting man who had made it big in the computer-aided gambling business. His name was Billy Walters, and he became Mickelson's intermediary for the golfer's sports betting hobby. The two men had a good friendship and a good business relationship, meaning that no questions were ever raised as to the legality of any betting exploits. No reason to believe otherwise has ever cropped up, but the insider trading scenario is a different story.

Walters had a long-time friend called Tom Davis, who was on the board of directors of a company called Dean Foods, a massive, nation-wide dairy processor. In the 1990s, Davis made significant amounts of money from Dean Foods, but he seemed to have a habit of gambling it away. Back then, Walters and Davis had been wealthy men, but in 2011, after a failed golf course purchase investment operation, the two fell on relatively hard times. A simple, yet very audacious, insider trading plan was hatched to pull themselves out of their deep financial hole.

There are two ways to make money through insider trading: by buying stocks that will increase or selling stocks that will decrease. These are the aims of stock market trading, but non-insiders do not know what the stocks will do. Walters and Davis had done something similar in 2008, when, as per Davis' instruction, Walters bought stock in Dean Foods. Davis knew that there was an increase on the horizon, and Walters ended up selling at a profit of roughly $6 million. The two pals carried on buying and selling on a semi-regular basis, and in 2012, Phil Mickelson was invited to join.

Davis knew that Dean Foods had a plan to launch a subsidiary called White Waves, which would undoubtedly send the stock value skyrocketing. Lefty bought stock, and a little more than a week later, he sold his shares, making just less than $1 million dollars, from which he paid Billy Walter to settle a gambling debt. The truth thereof was never confirmed, but it wouldn't have come as a surprise.

FBI investigators, who monitor the stock market in order to identify insider trading and other means of fraud, took an interest in Dean Foods. There was quite clearly something to it, and after two years of evidence building, two federal agents appeared at Davis' home for a chat about his associations with Walters. The discussion took place in May 2014, and Davis lied from then until the end of 2015, when he pleaded guilty to misleading the Securities and Exchange Commission as well as to insider trading. Davis was staring down nearly 200 years in prison as a maximum punishment, but by outing Walters and cooperating in the investigation, he was able to have a shot at taking a severely reduced sentence.

The prosecution team had a big decision to make: whether or not they had sufficient evidence to charge Phil Mickelson with insider trading. It was clear that significant money was made, but legal anomalies indicated that charges would perhaps not stick. Traditionally, insider trading involves two people: the one who provides the tip and the one who receives the tip and acts on it. In this case, those two people were Davis and Walters, respectively. This would make Mickelson a third party, as the information he received was from Walters and not Davis. If it was the case that Mickelson had had no contact with Davis, then the former would not be guilty of any crime. In the end, Billy Walters only got five years in possibly the most cushy prison in the United States, and Tom Davis got just two years. Mickelson never faced charges, but he did pay the Securities and Exchange Commission $1 million to avoid civil litigation. Lefty, who continues to thrill crowds with his charisma and skills, scraped that one by the skin of his teeth.

Jane Blalock Versus the LPGA

Jane Blalock learned golf and played professionally at a time when the women's game garnered little attention, but she was a golfer of acclaim. Her debut LPGA event was in 1969, and she retired in 1987. Blalock, christened Barbara but known by her middle name, Jane, has done a huge amount for the women's game, being the force behind the professional league for veteran female golfers. She is a Hall of Famer herself and holds the record for most wins on the LPGA without a major. It cannot be argued that she was one of the best women golfers around, but her playing days were not without controversy.

The Controversy

The LPGA had their eye on Blalock, leading to a three-year dispute between the golfer and the sanctioning body. It started in 1972, in Kentucky, when Blalock was disqualified from the LPGA Bluegrass Invitational for signing an incorrect scorecard. This is something that does happen from time to time, and most often it is an innocent mistake but a costly and frustration-rendering one. The disqualification came in the second round, despite Blalock's playing partners stating that the card was correct and that she had also signed it correctly. Suddenly, the offense changed, or was added to, as Blalock was cited for having moved her ball on at least one of the Kentucky greens. The usual protocol is to put a small round marker behind the ball, pick up the ball, and replace the ball before moving the marker. This is done for two reasons: firstly, if the ball is blocking the line of sight to the hole for other players, but also as an opportunity to clean the ball in order to prevent specks of dirt from altering its role during putting. A golfer cannot pick up the ball and place it back in a different, more favorable position, but this is what Blalock allegedly did. The usual punishment would have been a two-shot penalty, but word is that Blalock told officials that she would not be taking such a penalty.

In addition to being disqualified, Blalock was given a token fine of $500, and although there was confusion as to the initial assertions about the scorecard, Blalock's opponents were outraged. Over 20 LPGA players banded together and demanded a harsher punishment. In the wake thereof, an inquiry was held by the LPGA board of executors, and a decision to ban Blalock from golf for twelve months was taken. The board announced that Blalock had been under scrutiny for placing her ball back in different spots to improve her line for more than just a few tournaments. It was also stated that Blalock had admitted to having done so on numerous occasions. Blalock, on the other hand, defended herself publicly, claiming that she had never improved her line by placing a ball incorrectly and that she had never admitted to doing so.

In early June 1972, less than two weeks after being handed the year-long ban, Blalock pulled out all the stops by launching an appeal of sorts against the suspension. Her lawyers did so in the federal courts by way of a $5 million suit, demanding that the LPGA executives reverse their decision. Part of the argument was that Blalock's words were twisted into admissions and that she had never categorically stated that she did act illegally. It was alleged that the women on the LPGA tour who called for the harsher punishment were involved in a conspiracy to get rid of a competitor to improve their collective chances of winning more tournaments.

The presiding judge considered the fact that at the time, current active LPGA tour players sat as executives on the board and ruled that players could not make objective judgments on fellow players, as was the case with Blalock. There was never a finding of guilt or innocence, but appeals flew back and forth until 1975, when the LPGA and Blalock reached some form of mutual understanding through a settlement. Maybe Blalock should have just taken the two-shot penalty...

Lexi Thompson: The Ball Mover

A spectator made sure Lexi Thompson would be removed from a potentially tournament-winning position due to the improper replacement of her golf ball on the green. Thompson was playing at the 2017 edition of the Chevron Championship, at California's Mission Hills Country Club. As the fourth round got underway, Thompson was good for the win, but just before stepping onto the 13th tee, she was notified that a fan had emailed in an allegation that Thompson had illegally replaced her ball on the 17th green the day before. The officials had reviewed the footage and were in agreement with the meddling email sender, thus imposing a two-shot penalty. Another two shots were added to Thompson's score for signing an incorrect scorecard. Despite the penalties, Thompson finished tied for first with Ryu So-yeon and forced a sudden-death playoff, which the Korean won.

Was it Fair?

This is a double-barrelled question, because without the penalty, Thompson would have won; of that there is little doubt. Maybe the sanction was a fair one, but the LPGA letting a completely unaffiliated member of the public dictate to them is probably not aligned with fairness. The cynic might say that the only consideration is whether or not Thompson cheated, and the larger belief is that she did not. With every re-watch of the footage, one's mind sways back and forth as to whether the ball position was altered, but the resounding conclusion is that poor Thompson was not aware at all, and the infraction was a complete mistake. The cynic might again say that even though Thompson didn't cheat per se, the rules still had to be applied. At the end of the day, an "armchair" golfer pulled a dirty move that cost Thompson a huge win. One can imagine how difficult those last six holes were, especially seeing that Thompson's drive on the 13th was through teary eyes.

Australian Football League (AFL)

Very few people outside Australia seem to get AFL, or Aussie Rules, as it is also known. The players wear vests and shorts that are far too tight and involve themselves in some sort of soccer, rugby, and rugby league hybrid, where umpires make ridiculously rigid signals when points are scored. AFL and the National Rugby League (NRL) grapple with each other for the title of "most popular sport in Australia," but every now and then, stars turn into villains through a spot of illegal gambling.

Rhys Nicholls

During the 2021 AFL season, Nicholls placed 10 bets, 6 of which were on his own teams' games. The Gold Coast Suns player spent AUD 256 ($181), but proved either that he had too much faith in his team or that he was a terrible gambler, or maybe both. Nicholls lost every single bet but was still caught, and he had to pay a AUD 5,000 ($3,545) fine, totaling AUD 5,256 ($3,726). He also got a two-game suspension and a reminder that betting accounts in players' names cannot be used for AFL betting. Nicholls, who was 20 at the time, was fully compliant during questioning, and his team stood by him. However, one would suspect that he was the brunt of a few jokes, as the events were fairly innocuous in context.

Jaidyn Stephenson

Rhys Nicholls clearly didn't learn from Collingwood Football Club's Jaidyn Stephenson, who had done the same thing two seasons earlier. Stephenson proved to be just as bad at gambling as his future Gold Coast Suns punter, but Stephenson got off very lightly. His bets were all on his home team, with one on himself to kick a goal. The other two were on the winning spread and an out-and-out win. Stephenson lost AUD 36 ($26), and to add insult to injury, he received a 10-game suspension but no monetary penalty. One could argue that after this 2019 incident, sanctions were stepped up in order to stave off temptation, which is why Rhys Nichols was stung for AUD 5000 ($3,545).

Parting Shot

For an association that is so against gambling, a AUD 10 million ($6.9 million) sponsorship deal with BetEasy in 2020 may have raised an eyebrow or two.

The Snooker Cheats

Pool hustlers, and to a lesser degree, snooker players, have been around for as long as the game has. The old trick was to purposefully play badly against an opponent, then accept the challenge of an on-looker, only to bring out the A game, and claim the wager placed on the match up. Maybe the risk of being beaten up was the biggest of them all in small-time pub hustling, but in the big leagues, the ramifications of cheating are much harsher.

The Match-Fixers: Yu Delu and Cau Yupeng

The two Chinese professionals, who both showed huge promise as youngsters, made some serious errors of judgment. Things are a bit hazy as to how the men were actually outed, but it is known that the fixed matches are as follows:

Yu Delu:

- 2015 versus Martin McRuddin, during qualifiers for the Indian Open.
- 2015 versus Dominic Dale, Germany.
- 2016 versus Ian Glover, during the Welsh Open.
- 2017 versus Michael Georgiou, during qualifiers for the European Masters.
- 2017 versus Kurt Maflin, during the Shanghai Masters.

Cao Yupeng:

- 2016 versus Ali Carter, during the Welsh Open.
- 2016 versus Stuart Bingham, during qualifiers for the Indian Open.
- 2016 versus Stephen Maguire, during the UK Championship.

Cao, who reached a career high world ranking of 43, admitted everything and cooperated fully during the World Professional Billiards and Snooker Association's investigation. He admitted to receiving £5,000 GBP ($6,550) for each of the three games he fixed in 2016, and he expressed deep regret and regret.In exchange for his willing and apologetic behavior, his punishment was somewhat mitigated. Cao, who was 28 at the time of the 2018 hearings, was given a 6-year ban, with 6 years of suspension, and made his comeback in 2020.

Yu, on the other hand, initially lied to investigators and showed little remorse. He did eventually admit to fixing the 5 games and was given a big kick in the teeth by way of a 10 year and 9 month ban, as well as a £20,823.80 GBP ($27,279.18) fine.

Cao has subsequently become involved in the World Professional Billiards and Snooker Association's drive to educate young players about the dangers of fixing games and becoming involved in corruption. It goes to show that some players have regret, humility, and a desire to help other players avoid falling into the same trap.

Come Back Stephen Lee

Debates have raged for many years as to whether Stephen Lee should be allowed to come back to professional snooker, given that, at the time of this writing, he has served 10 years of his 12-year ban for gambling.

Some would say that the answer should be a resounding "no," given that his illegal activities continued after his ban. There have been two run-ins with the law; most recently, in 2018, he was nabbed by the Hong Kong police and charged with working on a tourist visa. Big Stephen had been coaching snooker, for which he was paid. He pleaded not guilty in April, at which time he had his passport confiscated. The trial was set to begin in June, and Lee changed his plea to guilty early on. He had to pay HK$1,000, or only £95 GBP ($126,35), and then got himself out of Hong Kong, post haste.

If we go back further to 2014, Lee sold his snooker cue as a memorabilia item over Facebook but never provided the buyer with the cue. He was fined £110 GBP ($146,30) and was ordered to return the £1,600 GBP ($2,128) that he had received from the cue buyer.

These two incidents were probably more stupid than anything else, and many believe they should not be included in the equation for reintroducing big Stephen into the game.

The Big Seven

Stephen Lee, a larger-than-life personality from the South West of England, was also a large man who, because of his weight, looked awkward around the snooker table. It didn't matter how he looked, though; Lee had a prolific career, reaching nine ranking finals and winning five of them. Success around the table was not enough for Lee, and his greed saw him accept a £40,000 GBP ($67,000) deal to throw seven matches during 2008 and 2009.

It was a match against Welshman Ryan Day at the 2009 World Championships that had tongues wagging. A quiet investigation took place by the gambling commission, which saw Lee arrested in early February 2010. Big Stephen was granted bail and continued on his way. Knowing he was guilty, Lee should have stopped there, and it is believed that he did for a while, but in October 2012, he threw a game against a Scotsman, John Higgins. The World Professional Billiards and Snooker Association sprung into action, and tip-offs from two unnamed bookies resulted in a ban for the former world number 5. No time period was stipulated, and it took some time for the matter to be set down before Sports Resolution UK, an independent tribunal appointed by the WPBSA.

The inquiry lasted three days only because Lee continued to deny the allegations. One week after the conclusion, he was found guilty of fixing games against Ken Doherty, Marco Fu, and Neil Robertson during the 2008 Malta Cup. At the UK Championship, also in 2008, Lee threw games against Stephen Hendry and Mark King, as well as against Mark Selby at the 2009 China Open. His 12-year ban, backdated to October 2012, was confirmed on September 25, 2013. Lee had been associated with more than one gambling ring and helped them win at least £95,000 GBP ($159,600). The £40,000 GBP ($67,000) reward was deposited into Lee's wife's bank account, but after several unsuccessful appeals, Lee was left out of pocket for £125,000 GBP ($210,000).

At the time of writing, Lee's 19-year-old son Alfie was looking certain to join the professional ranks. The sad part is that Lee will not be able to watch his son until October 12, 2024, as his ban includes attendance at any WPBSA-sanctioned effort. Twelve years is a long time, and maybe the WPBSA should allow a small indulgence by granting Lee the right to attend events as a spectator. Young Alfie Lee deserves to have his father as a supporter, one might argue.

John Higgins

Public opinion, especially among Stephen Lee fans, is that John Higgins should have been booted out of world snooker instead of getting a six-month ban and a £75,000 GBP ($117,000) fine. Higgins and his manager, Pat Moony, made a trip to Kiev, the capital of the Ukraine, in the first part of 2010. There was no tournament being hosted, and snooker had almost no popularity in the Eastern European country, so it was very strange when footage of John Higgins in Kiev emerged. He is seen shaking hands with known illegal gamblers as part of a gentleman's agreement to receive £260,000 GBP ($405,600) in exchange for losing frames.

The mitigating factor may be that it was frames and not matches, but one must remember that the reward was more than five times what Lee had received. Match-fixing charges were brought against Higgins and then dropped soon after. He was found guilty of violating the rules during a betting discussion and was given a short ban and a medium-sized fine. Higgins' manager was banned for life, which caused a lot of head scratching. One can only speculate that the gamblers used some of their loot to pay off the snooker powers that were in an effort to rescue Higgins. The WPBSA would certainly argue otherwise, but anything is possible.

NHL Cheating Scandals

Ice hockey is a mix of gloves from boxing, heavily padded men wearing skates, and a disc-looking object called a puck that is slapped with flat sticks across the ice, from player to player, and into the goal. Mostly referred to as "hockey," it has been widely acknowledged as Canada's national winter sport. The Americans also get involved in what is known as the National Hockey League, which was rocked by a scandal that broke in 2006.

Operation Slapshot

A well-known Philadelphia-based crime family, the Bruno-Scarfos, were at the center of this controversy, accused of their participation in an illegal gambling syndicate. Their exact role was unclear, and they may not have been involved at all, but evidence of over 1,000 illegal wagers, totaling more than $1.7 million, was uncovered. The bets were on professional and college sports, but it appeared that ice hockey did not feature, as the sports gambled on were football and basketball.

Wayne Gretzky, the most famous hockey player of all time, had his name dragged into the scandal, as his wife Janet had been placing bets in some form or another. It was media sensationalism and amounted to nothing, but the real culprits were James Ulmer, Rick Tocchet, and James Harney.

State trooper Harney alleged that he and Tocchet, the Phoenix Coyotes' assistant coach at the time, were 50–50 partners in running the illegal operation. James Ulmer, a New Jersey businessman, had slightly less involvement and cooperated with investigators in return for a reduced prison sentence. He pleaded guilty to conspiracy and promoting gambling. It turned out that he didn't go to prison at all, although the presiding judge told him that he would be put behind bars if he did not stay out of trouble for two years. It was a bit of a strange thing to say, indicative that Ulmer could start getting himself into trouble after 24 months and 1 day, but that isn't what he actually meant. Harney pleaded guilty to conspiracy, promoting gambling, and official misconduct and received a five-year prison sentence. Tocchet, who actually participated in Operation Slapshot, made a wise decision to do so, as he was handed down a two-year probation period.

The interesting part was that none of the participants were found to be placing bets on hockey; they just happened to be involved in hockey as well as illegal gambling on other sports. Some observers found it comical that the secret investigation had the same name as a type of shot played hundreds of times in every hockey game, and just like that, the NHL carried on, seemingly untainted.

The Danish Hockey Cheats

When one thinks of Denmark, ice hockey is probably not the first sport that comes to mind, but it is relatively popular. The players don't make the kind of money offered in the NHL, which could be a reason behind the match-fixing exploits of Dennis Jensen, Kiril Starkov, and Tyler Mosienko.

Jensen, the second-string goalkeeper for Esbjerg, came up with the plan and invited his two teammates to join him. The match in question was against Rungsted Hockey in January 2014, and Jensen placed a bet on his opponents to score one goal or more in the first period. It was for Starkov and Mosienko, from Canada, to ensure that it happened. When Jensen found out that he was going to start the game, which wasn't a common occurrence, he placed another bet on Rungsted scoring two or more goals in the first period.

Rungsted scored three goals in the first period, and Jensen must have breathed a sigh of relief. However, that relief wouldn't last long, as regular keeper Ervin Mustukovs suspected something was amiss. Jensen had previously approached Mustukovs, asking him to let goals in purposefully for Jensen's betting success.

Starkov and Mosienko got off with mild sentences, having to pay fines of 12,000 Danish kroner ($2,236) and 4,000 kroner ($735), respectively, as well as sit on the sidelines for five games each. Jensen, who played the biggest part, was suspended for a full year and had to pay a fine of 12,000 kroner, about $2,343. Jensen's overall loss, via his fine and his would-be earnings, amounted to more than five times his betting proceeds. a strong sense of regret, one would imagine.

The Harding Versus Kerrigan Rivalry Turned Ugly

Imagine what it would be like if you were an honest, hardworking, committed athlete with a dream of Olympic gold that was destroyed in a violent, selfish manner by associates of your great rival. Well, this scenario played out in the world of ice skating. This scandal is one of the biggest of all time, and it was terribly executed by individuals that should have used some common sense.

Tonya Harding

Ice skating is one of those sports in which you must begin early if you want to pursue a professional career. An American figure skater by the name of Johnny Weir started at age 12, which is considered a very late start, and is one skater among a handful that have gone on to have a professional career with such a late start in the context of the sport. Tonya Harding started at age three, in 1974, but didn't get off to the best start in life. She grew up very poor with a deadbeat dad who struggled to hold down a job and an abusive mother who supported the family. Despite the physical attacks and psychological outbursts, Mrs. Harding still had some sort of love for her daughter, as she paid for everything figure skating-related. One could argue that it was a selfish attempt to make Tonya a success and live vicariously through her. In addition, Tonya was sexually abused by a stepbrother, who was jailed but released without charge on the insistence of Tonya's mother.

Nancy Kerrigan

Kerrigan got a slightly later start than Harding. Her older brothers played ice hockey, and Kerrigan would hang around the rink with her parents. She wasn't particularly interested in hockey but liked the skating part and started taking group lessons at age six. Like Harding, Kerrigan grew up poor but in a household with lots of love, willing to make sacrifices in order to give their only daughter a shot at achieving her dreams.

The Rivalry

As Harding and Kerrigan progressed through the amateur ranks, a competitive but respectful rivalry started to grow. As professionals, 1991 saw the two figure skaters face each other in multiple events. Harding had a slightly better year than Kerrigan, winning silver over Kerrigan's bronze at the World Championships hosted in Germany and claiming gold at the U.S. Championships. Harding, who became the first woman in history to successfully land a triple axel, also won the 1994 U.S. Championships, but this time her long-time rival was not competing.

The Attack

On January 6, 1994, Nancy Kerrigan was skating in a practice session at the Cobo Arena in Detroit. After the session, while Kerrigan was walking off the ice but still in the arena, an assailant with a heavy-duty baton smashed Kerrigan's knee, leaving her sprawled on the ground in a fury of tears, pain, and shock. The aftermath was caught on film, which allowed Kerrigan's attacker to be identified, but he had achieved his goal. Due to the attack, Kerrigan was unable to compete in the U.S. National Championships, which took place the next night in Minneapolis. Harding's victory secured her a place at the Olympic Games in Norway's city of Lillehammer, starting on February 12. Due to the circumstances, Kerrigan still made the Olympic team and took home the silver medal, with Harding securing eighth place.

The Culprits

The man who performed the attack was called Shane Stant, who allegedly received a reward of $6,500. The masterminds were Harding's ex-husband, Jeff Gillooly, and her bodyguard, Shawn Echardt. The latter owned up, and by doing so, he incriminated Stant, Gillooly, and the getaway car driver, Derrick Smith, an uncle of Stant's. Questions were being asked about Harding's possible involvement, but she convincingly denied that she was part of the plot and stated that she had no knowledge of it.

Gillooly was quick to name Harding as one of the conspirators, and her claims of innocence were not assisted by the discovery of written notes detailing Kerrigan's practice schedule. A handwriting expert found that the notes had been penned by Harding. Despite the finding, Harding was insistent that she had nothing to do with the incident. With the discovery of further evidence and increased pressure on Harding, she pleaded guilty on March 16, 1994.

The Punishments

All four men received prison time for charges including assault, conspiracy to commit assault, and racketeering. Gillooly was sentenced to two years, while Eklardt, Stant, and Smith got 18 months each. The attack was incredibly amateurish, with little effort made to conceal it and no planning or consideration of consequences. Harding initially appeared to be the second victim, but sadly, the victimhood was turned around very quickly. Harding didn't go to prison but was given three years' probation, a life ban, and a $160,000 fine.

The 2002 Winter Olympics Figure Skating Scandal

A scandal has to be pretty big to have a documentary made about it, and this scandal has two: meddling and bad sport (*episode four*). Any sport where points judging is involved opens itself up to subjectivity, but the idea is to judge completely on the quality of the competitor within the rules and framework of the event.

What Actually Happened?

In the 2002 Salt Lake City Winter Olympics pairs figure skating competition, the proper order was not followed. Before the scores were revealed, the event commentators declared the Canadian husband-and-wife team, David Pelletier and Jamie Sale, gold medal winners. To their absolute dismay, the scores reflected that the Russian pair, Anton Sikharulidze and Elena Berezhnaya, had ousted the Canadians into second place.

The press was all over it, and rumors arose that the French judge had picked the Russians as winners at the behest of a Russian mobster, Alimzhan Tokhtakhounov. That turned out to be untrue when Tokhtakhounov was released without being charged after a later arrest in Italy. The other story was that a French ice-skating administrator had instructed his country's women and judge, Marie-Reine Le Cougne, to vote for the Russians in order to assist the French pair in the upcoming ice dance part of the competition. The second story turned out to be true, and the French judge and administrator, Didier Gailhaguet, were given three-year suspensions and barred from attending the next Olympic Games, but not before the Canadian pair were retrospectively awarded gold medals. The Russians still got to keep their gold and attend the ceremony a second time, as for the first time in history it was repeated.

The result

The judging system had been in need of a change for a long time, and the incident resulted in scores being kept secret. Not the best idea, considering that it became easier to cheat due to the anonymity.

Abortion Doping

As outrageous as it sounds, there is reason to believe that female athletes in the past have engaged in becoming purposefully pregnant and terminating the pregnancy. The result is similar to EPO use because, in the first trimester, the hormones produced cause a spike in red blood cells. Rumor has it that Soviet athletes used this method at the 1956 Melbourne Olympics and the 1964 Tokyo Olympics. A statistic not backed up by any evidence is that 10 medal winners had participated in abortion doping.

Suspicions

It seems as though no conclusive proof has been uncovered, but suspicions do exist, although they are relatively murky and anonymous in nature.

The "Fake" Confession

Olga Kovalenko, a 1968 Olympic gold medal-winning Soviet gymnast, announced during an interview after her retirement that she had participated in abortion doping. Kovalenko later announced that the newspaper that published the interview had faked it all. The announcement seemed credible, as Kovalenko had succeeded in a defamation lawsuit against the newspaper.

The Verdict

It does seem outrageous, but considering the evils of the Soviet Union in the Cold War era, it could be true, and also near impossible to prove.

The Rugby Union Bloodgate Scandal

Rugby union is a sport that has managed to fly under the radar when it comes to match-fixing scandals. There have been rumblings in the past, but nothing major has really come to the fore. One could say that rugby union has been clean, or at least relatively so, since young William Webb Ellis picked up a football and ran with it during a game at Rugby School, Rugby, England, in 1823. Bloodgate tarnished the game slightly, but it was forgotten nearly as fast as it happened.

The Substitution Rule

If we go far enough back in rugby history, there was a time where players could only be substituted if they sustained an injury serious enough to prevent them from carrying on. This is the reason why competitors used to play through pulled muscles, bleeding faces, and concussions. Modern rugby allows up to eight replacements, partially for injury but also tactically. Often several of the substitutes will run on sometime during the mid to latter part of the second half, fresh and raring to go, as per the game plan. Once substituted, you cannot come back unless a substitute in the front row gets injured or there is a blood injury.

What Happened?

The Irish provincial side Leinster was facing Harlequins in the 2009 Heineken Cup quarterfinal at a packed Stoop Stadium in Twickenham, England. Both sides had strong desires to win, but one of the sides was prepared to do it illegally. All-Black international Nick Evans was injured seven minutes into the second half and was replaced by Chris Malone of Australia. Malone, a goalkicker of acclaim, as was Evans, also picked up an injury with about 10 minutes remaining in the match. Harlequins were left with no recognized kicker, and the only way they stood a shot of winning was to score points, via a try or a kick, the latter being more likely. Getting Nick Evans back on was their last hope, but the only way it could happen was if a blood injury occurred. Evans was spotted warming up, which was odd but didn't raise suspicion at the time. The next thing, Tom Williams was being led off the field with blood pouring from his mouth, which allowed Evans to return. The New Zealander, who was struggling to walk, ended up taking a kick, which he duly missed. It was blindingly obvious that there was something dodgy going on, and initial thoughts were that Williams must have intentionally butted heads with either a teammate or opponent to get a bloody cut. What actually happened was the use of a vat of fake blood from a party shop, which traditionally would be used as part of a Halloween getup.

Leinster smelled a rat, and their team doctor went to the Harlequins' changing room to investigate. Dean Richards, director of rugby at Harlequins, was in the changeroom with Williams and Dr. Wendy Chapman, the doctor who looked after the Harlequins players. Before the Leinster doctor entered and under the instructions of Richards, Wendy Chapman cut Tom Williams' lip to make it appear as if the injury was real. Nobody was fooled, and in a cowardly move, Dean Richards resigned amidst Leinster celebrations.

The Punishment

The Rugby Football Union, England's governing body, got to work, and investigations revealed what everyone already knew. The man who was sent to buy the fake blood vat and tasked with slipping it to Williams was the Harlequins team physio, Steph Brennan, who was banned from rugby for two years but only served one. Dean Richards, the orchestrator and director of rugby, got a three-year ban. Tom Williams got twelve months, which were later reduced to four. Dr. Chapman also got 12 months but was permitted to return to private practice.

Harlequins escaped suspension or expulsion but were slapped with a €300,000 ($417,000) fine, and in a completely unrelated incident, the fake blood supply shop, Party Superstore, was burned down two years later. An unfair dose of karma, as the shopkeeper had absolutely nothing to do with bloodgate.

The 1995 Rugby World Cup Poisoning Scandal

The All Blacks, New Zealand's international rugby union team, have been a formidable force in world rugby almost since the Brits took the game to the small South Pacific island in the 1800s. The All Blacks are the most successful sports team in history, with a winning percentage of just over 77% as measured over more than 100 years of competition (Smythe, 2017). During the 1995 Rugby World Cup Final, the team's odds were not in their favor when they lost to South Africa's Springboks at Ellis Park Stadium in

Johannesburg on a warm winter afternoon. Two days earlier, on June 22, most of the All Blacks squad found themselves projectile vomiting in a manner consistent with eating undercooked meat. It started at a movie theater and continued at the team hotel, but come Saturday, June 24, the players were all fine, bar winger Jeff Wilson, who retired from the game at halftime.

Prior to the loss, nobody in the New Zealand camp had mentioned the Thursday night incidents; however, after the tournament, they became public. Accusations were leveled at the South Africans for orchestrating the poisoning, but they never amounted to anything, and the rumblings died down quickly, allowing the Springboks to attend ticker-tape parades and revel in the glory of being world champions. Maybe one has to give credit to the New Zealand camp for not making a big deal about it, and it seems commonly agreed upon that the Springboks had nothing to do with it. Either a case of an outside influence or perhaps just a case of genuine, unfortunately timed food poisoning.

The Fog Jockey

A jockey starts a race, leading his horse off the track, hiding in the fog, and rejoining ahead of the pack on the second lap. It sounds like a cartoon, but it actually happened. Landing Gear, ridden by Sylvester Carmouche Jr., won the mile-long race at Delta Downs Racetrack in Louisiana on January 11 by an absurdly large margin of about 24 lengths. Landing Gear was examined after finishing, as is the protocol, and the Louisiana Racing Commission vet immediately picked up that the thoroughbred had not just run a mile-long race. Like so many cheats, Carmouche Jr. failed to think that he might get caught, but I am sure even he will admit that it was a terrible plan. The humiliated jockey was banned for 10 years, fined $250 plus court costs, and sent to jail for 30 days, but managed to spend only 10 days behind bars due to 20 days being suspended by the judge. There is no doubt that it didn't take all 10 days to develop a deep sense of regret.

Boris the Cheat

The modern pentathlon is a somewhat obscure sporting event, as it combines cross-country running, show jumping, swimming, shooting, and fencing. There is just such diversity across the five disciplines that being able to participate at the highest level in an event so diverse is admirable in itself. Boris Onishenko, a Soviet communist later dubbed "Boris the Cheat," was a superstar of the sport. He won 11 medals at the World Championships in team and individual events, 5 of which were gold. In addition, Onishenko won a team silver medal in the 1968 Olympics and a team gold medal in the 1972 Olympics, with an individual silver in 1972, completing his tally of three.

Onishenko could have taken home more Olympic medals, but in 1976, at the Moscow Games, he was caught cheating in the fencing section of the modern pentathlon. In fencing, there is a cord from the body to an electrical box, and a light flashes when you are touched by the tip of the weapon. Onishenko very cleverly manipulated the electronics by adding a switch that would short the circuit and cause the light to flash, even though his weapon had not made contact. The British team, who went on to win gold, cried foul, and the altered weapon was discovered, meaning that Onishenko was disqualified, leaving his team one man short and with no choice but to withdraw.

Boris the Cheat was handed a life ban, which was no doubt embarrassing, but he was 38 years old and nearing the end of his career anyway, so he wasn't robbed of much competition. He also had his awards and rank stripped before being swiftly kicked out of the Communist Party. His next chosen line of work was as a taxi driver in Kyiv, where he probably wowed many clients with his unique story.

Dora Ratjen

As a teenager, German-born Dora Ratjen narrowly missed out on a silver medal in the women's high jump in front of her home crowd at the 1936 Berlin Olympic Games. Two years later, in 1938, Ratjen broke the world record, formerly held by British athlete Dorothy Odam. It was an unfortunate situation; Ratjen was intersex due to having both male and female sexual organs. In the mid- to late 1930s, little was known about the condition, but Ratjen was registered as a girl and raised as one. When Ratjen was about 11 years old, she told her parents that she was a boy, but she was still forced to dress in girls' clothing and be seen as a girl by her mother and father.

Several months after having broken the women's high jump world record, Ratjen's sex was questioned by the police. Ratjen had been accused of being a man dressed as a woman while riding a train in Austria. She was subjected to medical and criminal investigations, and she was officially classified as a man, but she was never charged with fraud. Ratjen's sex was officially changed to "male" at the Bremen Registry Office, and he was ordered to return his silver medal in addition to being stripped of the world record. He was then sent to Hanover, where he worked in a bar. Ratjen was requested for interviews on many occasions but declined on every occasion. It can be put down to a sad situation in a time when little was known about intersex births, but there did not seem to be any actual intention to cheat, maybe just some internal turmoil and confusion.

Chapter 10

Countering the Cheats

It is safe to say that cheating in sports will never be eliminated completely. There are too many creative ways to cheat, and even more creative ways to get away with it. The abundance of television cameras at sporting events makes it difficult to be an "on-field," "on-track," or "in-arena" cheat. However, a lot of the cheating goes on behind closed doors, and as long as sports exist, there will be nefarious behavior, mainly motivated by money or an insatiable desire to win. The fight against cheating is ongoing, and it amounts to plugging holes as a prevention measure, then looking for the next hole to plug. But it would be wonderful to watch a sport with unflagging confidence that it is clean in every aspect.

The Perfect Game

To some, a "perfect game" is defined as flawless execution of skill and ability to win. To others, the perfect game means the perfect cheat, especially when there is big money involved. Efforts are being made to make the first interpretation more prevalent than the latter, and that is at least a start.

Fix the Fixing Project

Sometimes in politics and in the politics of sport, "save face" projects are used to forgive offenders and dull the impact of contentious events. The Fix the Fixing Project doesn't quite fit into those categories, but one may question how effective it actually is. The project is based on match-fixing education, but to be fair, how much does one need to know? Nobody who has cheated, attempted to cheat, gambled illegally, or fixed matches has been unaware that they are doing something morally wrong and often against the law. The project runs courses and conferences that teach administrators, players, and athletes about things they probably already know, but hey, at least they are trying to do something.

Together Against Match-Fixing (TAMF)

The Dutch Football League (DFL) and the German Football Association collaborated on this initiative, which is similar to the Fix the Fixing Project. Together Against Match-Fixing runs online workshops, available to only the Bundesliga and two Bundesliga senior and youth teams. Considering that football is a global sport, the project isn't very inclusive, but its website can be accessed by anyone. The website sets out sporting and legal rules, Ombudsman details, complaint procedures, and the dangers of gambling addiction, specifically in e-football. One can't help but question if the project is actually achieving anything, but if it prevents some cheating here and there, then one would conclude that it is achieving something.

What Else Can Be Done?

It depends on the sport, but it comes down to keeping a closer eye on the repetition of tactics that have been used in the past. More frequent drug testing, closer examinations of equipment, and sanctions that are equivalent to the offense. Perhaps life bans for anyone involved in any cheating, gambling, or match-fixing, no matter what sport and no matter how serious the offense. Even if that becomes the norm, cheating, gambling, and match fixing will never go away, but neither will sports fans either.

Conclusion

Why do people play sports?

Well, it depends on who you ask. To the once-a-month golfer, it is a form of non-competitive fun or maybe even competitive fun. A Sunday league cricket match may not have a big prize or much acclaim, but it can still have fierce competition. The feeling of victory shared with 10 friends is the reward. A loss still hurts, but it is a part of sports that has to be accepted. A middle-of-the-field marathon runner finds fulfillment in competing with him or herself to set a new personal best. Playing one-on-one basketball at the park is an event for bragging rights, and an amateur indoor football league is about comradery and the beers after the game.

The less competitive amongst us may go for mountain bike rides to escape life for a while and to keep fit. Some people find fulfillment in taking out their frustrations on a punching bag after work and imagining themselves as Tyson or Mayweather. However, for the amateur sportsman or woman, enjoyment is a major factor. Through sport, we learn life lessons, achieve fulfillment, and make lasting connections with others. Remember that only a tiny percentage of the world's population will be able to play professionally, and it is the best of the best that take up that mantle, chasing glory and wealth. An even smaller percentage of those fortunate enough to play professionally are cheaters or will become cheaters, and this leaves us amateurs feeling let down, disappointed, and angry. These scandals can prompt one to question sport and the damage done by cheats, gamblers, and match-fixers to their various athletic crafts.

In modern times, we may be forgiven for thinking that the cheating scandals going back over one hundred years were less significant. Speculation may say that the Black Sox fixing saga was not that bad, given that World War I had just ended and the feminist movement demanded more attention. Furthermore, 1919 is a long time ago, and it is difficult to contextualize the tarnishment of the game that the eight Chicago men facilitated. If we go back even further, this time in the cycling world of the early twentieth century, incidents like Hippolyte Aucouturier getting pulled along on his bike via a cork and a piece of string tied to a car in order to win the 1903 Tour de France are more humorous than lasting smears on the integrity of the sport.

On the subject of cycling, a good 90 or so years ago, the likes of Marco Pantani and Jan Ulrich put a dent in the sport's popularity with their involvement in doping. The Italian was a victim, and his premature death alone in a hotel room possibly deflected attention from doping. The German, Ulrich, seemed to take his doping efforts and the bans in stride, but at the time everyone in cycling knew that the practice was rife, and there may have been another small dent. Most people didn't lose faith in cycling despite these happenings, but it was a different story when cancer hero Lance Armstrong and his crew were busted. Cycling took a massive knock, and people turned their backs on the sport, labeling it a cheating circus endemic with dopers. But those people came back; they always do, and the message is that no matter how huge, outrageous, and far-reaching a scandal is, the sport as a whole always recovers...always!

Take soccer and the Golden Boy, Diego Maradona, who so charmingly and expertly described his illegal but still-awarded goal as "a little with the head of Maradona and a little with the hand of God." The incident took the world of soccer by storm, but it went away and the public decided to either forget it or at least move on. Italian football and the illegal betting rings run by the mob, or the 1971 German Bundesliga match-fixing scandal, or the 2020 Ukrainian ghost games, or Kim Christensen physically moving the goalposts, all created outcries, but the sport is just too vast in every aspect to be tarnished for very long. For soccer fans, even when a hero lets us down, a betting bribe is revealed, or there is a scandal involving the team that we scream for week in and week out, we do not lose that deep love for the beautiful game.

Of course, some scandals turn people off a sport forever, especially when an apparently honest, committed, and admirable player like Hansie Cronje is revealed as a greedy, manipulating cheat. Cronje was in a position of privilege in South African cricket, but his desire to make money got the best of him, and spot-fixing was so easy. He could persuade a player to score fewer than a certain number of runs while still winning the game with his conscience intact. It didn't go that way for long, and even though spot-fixing had been on the periphery of cricket for a while, Cronje shone a worldwide light on the extent of it. Many cricket fans turned their backs on Cronje and his fellow conspirators as they emerged one by one, but time heals all wounds. It happened again in Pakistan, in the IPL, and even in county cricket. The plots are always similar: the culprits are shamed, shockwaves shoot through the cricket community, and it all goes away. Cricket's popularity keeps growing as the T20 phenomenon stretches across countries that didn't even play the game when Hansiegate broke. The reality is that scandals have happened, do happen, and will happen in the future. However, they are specks of dust in the world of cricket, and the tarnish is temporary. The game triumphs over the few that cheat, and it is just too big to be significantly harmed.

Then you have boxing, which has been associated with betting from the beginning, but boxing is unique in that it takes place in casino arenas. Fighters go for months, even years, without stepping out in front of a crowd. They spend their time in gyms with trainers, preparing for world title bouts. There is no league or ongoing competition, but the paydays are huge, and it would seem that gambling is just part of the sport. The New York scene was run by the mob, and everyone knew that very little was above board. Even as the sport progressed through time, it may have cleaned itself up a little bit, but one would venture to say that boxing is not capable of much tarnishing, and two men facing off in the most primal way of settling a dispute will never ever lose its appeal. The thing is that gambling and fixing fights don't physically hurt anyone, but Tyson biting a part of Holyfield's ear right off and Luis Resto tampering with his gloves to such an extent that he nearly killed a man are acts of inexcusable violence that cannot be tolerated. Still, the fans come back.

Gambling is endemic in basketball, and getting paid for shaving points proved impossible to resist for college and NBA players alike. Even well-paid referees like Tim Donaghy got themselves involved with very rich and powerful men who just wanted more, more, more. One may argue that football scandals have leaned more towards cheating to win. No football fan will forget Tom Brady's deflated football endeavors, making them easier to throw, or Spygate, where young Matt Estrella was coerced into reading signals of other teams and communicating them to the New England Patriots coaches. Gambling hasn't been absent from football, as the Calvin Ridley and Brian Flores sagas showed us. However, Americans love their baseball and they love their football, and that countrywide love will never die. Smears on integrity, like in most other sports, don't hang around for protracted periods in the U.S.

Formula One is markedly different from other sports, and although drivers have to be fit, doping is something that has been steered clear of. Most scandals, of which there have been few compared to other sports, have been more about the manipulation of rules in schemes that have been frowned upon but not illegal. Cases in point would be Piquet and Rossburg's water-cooled braking scheme and BAR's extra fuel tank installation. On the illegal side, Piquet's son crashed tactically to get the safety car out, allowing Fernando Alonso to claw his way into first place. On the Nascar side of motorsport, races happen so often that cheating scandals are forgotten or pushed to the back of the mind relatively quickly. However, some of the ingenuity has to be admired. Like Formula 1, illegal gambling and doping haven't had an impact, but men like Smokey Yunick certainly have. He was a rule bender, not a rule breaker, and evidence of that was his three-and-a-half-meter fuel line and his method of putting cold fuel into his tank, knowing that it would expand as the car warmed up. He can't be called a cheat because he did nothing illegal. From Jeremy Mayfield's alleged methamphetamine use to Denny Hamilton and Ken Shrader's illegal modifications to Richard Petty's tyre swap, Nascar seems to enjoy a good scandal. It would be fair to say that the public enjoys the atmosphere, the noise, and the excitement of cars flying around a track and doesn't care too much about anything else.

It is safe to say that most gambling, cheating, and fixing schemes were thought out to some degree, but either way, they all seem to come out. However, the cynic would say that there must be dozens that have been disguised well enough to allow the perpetrators to get away with them. That is probably true, but we cannot forget the schemes that were so poorly planned or shortsighted enough to guarantee that they would never succeed.

Rosie Ruiz, the woman who did not have the build of a long distance athlete and who not so surreptitiously jumped out of a crowd so close to the finish of the Boston Marathon, crossed the line fresh, with no fatigue displayed. Ruiz ignored so many variables, like not being seen at all on the route by officials or spectators, and that the other competitors would not raise the fact that she hadn't passed them during the race. She also didn't take into account that she beat her winning time in the New York Marathon by almost half an hour. The indication was that she had cheated in that race too, but on top of her poorly thought out cheating scheme, she went on to get involved in cocaine deals and corporate fraud, which she was equally bad at. There was no smear left on marathon running or a tarnished reputation—just a woman who made herself a laughing stock.

Another laughable but equally upsetting scandal was the Nancy Kerrigan affair. The man who attempted to kick Kerrigan out of the Olympics did so in full view of television cameras. Apart from the lack of thought there, the plan backfired when Kerrigan medaled at the Olympics, leaving Tonya Harding floundering in eighth position. Similar to Ruiz, Harding and her co-conspirators didn't tarnish ice skating but did seriously embarrass themselves.

In addition to the poorly planned scandals, you get the bizarre. Abortion doping, Dora Ratjen competing as a woman, and Aussie Rules betting so unsuccessfully that the players lost their money and also got fined Bloodgate almost seems unreal, with a vat of fake blood from a party shop and a limping kicker who missed the vital kick anyway. The double standards like Stephen Lee getting banned for 12 years, even though his fixes were not as bad as John Higgins', who got 6 months.

The point that screams out way louder than any scandal in sporting history is that sport is monumentally larger than the cheats, gamblers, and match-fixers. Their activities are temporary, but sport is eternal. It was here before we were born, and it will be here after we die.

So now what?

Well, nothing changes. We will continue to discuss sports in the stands, at the pub, in our lounges, and anywhere else. The topics of the conversations will be skills, selection policies, underdog victories, rule changes, and innovations. We will continue with kick-arounds in the park, Sunday league cricket, and shouting at the referee from our armchairs. Sport will continue to teach us lessons, but we already know right from wrong. Of course cheating is terrible, and of course we wish it were not part of sports, but it is, and it remains an interesting subject that kindred spirits through sports will always include in conversation.

Always try to remember this apt quote from Knute Rockne, a Norwegian-born American football coach: One man practicing sportsmanship is far better than 50 preaching it (Rockne n.d.).

Authors Note

Thank you for reading this book!

If you enjoyed it and have a minute to spare, I would really appreciate a short review on the page or site where you bought the book.

Reviews from readers like you make a huge difference.

Thank you again!

DC

References

Hopps, D. (2000, May 25). *Malik Banned for Life as Pakistan Blows the Whistle.* https://www.theguardian.com/sport/2000/may/25/cricket

Beasely, A. (2021, June 1). *The Hansie Cronje Match Fixing Scandal.* https://www.gambling.com/news/the-hansie-cronje-match-fixing-scandal-the-complete-story-2241300

Blitz, M. (2015, March 23). *The Infamous 1951 CCNY Point Shaving Scandal.* http://www.todayifoundout.com/index.php/2015/03/infamous-1951-ccny-point-shaving-scandal/

Marsh, J. (2015, March 23). *The "Ghost Game" Phenomenon.* https://www.sportsintegrityinitiative.com/the-ghost-game-phenomenon/#:~:text=Ghost%20games%20are%20so%2Dcalled,reported%20to%20have%20been%20played.

Nicholson, P. (2020, March 31). *Ukraine "Ghost" Games Fool Bookies and Punters as Criminals Pull off Perfect Crime.* https://www.insideworldfootball.com/2020/03/31/ukraine-ghost-games-fool-bookies-punters-data-firm-criminals-pull-off-perfect-crime/

Blitz, M. (2015, March 23). *The Infamous 1951 CCNY Point Shaving Scandal.* http://www.todayifoundout.com/index.php/2015/03/infamous-1951-ccny-point-shaving-scandal/

Meuller, C. (2022, November 15). 110%. *The Greatest Hustle Plays in Sports History.* https://www.yardbarker.com/general_sports/articles/110_the_greatest_hustle_plays_in_sports_history/s1__32069177#slide_1

Richardson, J. (2019, February 2). *9 of the World's Greatest Pool Hustlers.* https://www.gamblingsites.net/blog/9-of-the-worlds-greatest-pool-hustlers/

Strackbein, N. (2022, August 2). *Steelers Brian Flores Responds to Dolphins Punishment for Tanking.* https://www.si.com/nfl/steelers/news/pittsburgh-steelers-brian-flores-miami-dolphins-punishmment-tanking

AAP. (2000, August 29). *Gibbs and Williams Banned For Six Months.* https://www.espncricinfo.com/story/gibbs-and-williams-banned-for-six-months-85609

Spekter, M. (2012, October 11). *Daily Comment:* It's Not About the Bike. https://www.newyorker.com/news/daily-comment/its-not-about-the-bike

Bowers, L. (2012, October 12). *How Did Lance Armstrong Avoid a Positive Doping Test?* https://www.livescience.com/23932-lance-armstrong-doping-tests.html

Unknown. (2013, March 3). *Lance Armstrong's Doctor Speaks Out For the First Time.* https://www.aljazeera.com/news/2013/3/3/lance-armstrongs-doctor-speaks-out-for-first-time

Schoener, B. Borger, J. (2022, May 1). *Continuing Education Activity:* Erythropoietin Stimulating Agents. https://www.ncbi.nlm.nih.gov/books/NBK536997/

Unknown. (2019, April 11). B*lood Doping and EPO:* An Anti-Doping FAQ. https://www.usada.org/spirit-of-sport/education/blood-doping-epo-faq/

Schaal, E. (2021, January 22). *Goodfellas:* The Real "Jimmy the Gent" Was Even More Vicious Than Robert De Niro's Version. https://www.cheatsheet.com/entertainment/goodfellas-the-real-jimmy-the-gent-was-even-more-vicious-than-robert-de-niros-version.html/

Times, H. (2010, November 3). Cronje Offered to Fix Match in 1996, Says Gibbs. https://www.hindustantimes.com/india/cronje-offered-to-fix-match-in-1996-says-gibbs/story-20Ss18QnNZY50Br5j46C2O.html

AAP. (2000, August 29). *Gibbs and Williams Banned For Six Months.* https://www.espncricinfo.com/story/gibbs-and-williams-banned-for-six-months-85609

Moonda, F. (2019, October 18). *Gulam Bodi Sentenced to Five Years in Prison.* https://www.espncricinfo.com/story/gulam-bodi-sentenced-to-five-years-in-prison-1204084

Florio, M. (2022, August 11). *Bruce Beal is Likely Out as Next Dolphin's Owner.* https://profootballtalk.nbcsports.com/2022/08/11/bruce-beal-is-likely-out-as-next-dolphins-owner/

Ward, J. (2006, September 19). *A Brief History of Zimbabwe Cricket.* https://www.espncricinfo.com/story/a-brief-history-of-zimbabwe-cricket-259980

Richter, F. (2022, July 25). *Has Pro Cycling Cleaned Up Its Act?* https://www.statista.com/chart/27716/share-of-tour-de-france-riders-convicted-of-doping/

Weston, A. (2022, November 15). *History of Online Gambling.* https://www.gamblingsites.com/history/

Smith, JB. (Unknown). *Baseball History, Origins, Growth and Changes in the Game.* https://www.thepeoplehistory.com/baseballhistory.html

Coatess, A. Hunter, S. (2022, November 15). *How Many Countries Play Baseball in 2022.* https://wezen-ball.com/how-many-countries-play-baseball/

Baker, K. (2021, April 6). *Almost a Third of MLB Players Were Born Outside the U.S.* https://www.axios.com/2021/04/06/mlb-baseball-rosters-foreign-born-players

Tylicki, D. (2011, November 18). *MLB History:* 20 Most Shocking Scandals in Baseball History. https://bleacherreport.com/articles/941589-20-most-shocking-scandals-in-baseball-history

Andrews, E. (2014, October 9). *What was the 1919 "Black Sox" Baseball Scandal?* https://www.history.com/news/black-sox-baseball-scandal-1919-world-series-chicago

Brothers, H. (2022, Unknown). *Dollar Times:* Calculate the Value. https://www.dollartimes.com/inflation/inflation.php?amount=100000&year=1919

Sutelin, E. (2021, October 29). *Astros Cheating Scandal Explained:* How Houson's Sign-Stealing Shook Up MLB. https://www.sportingnews.com/us/mlb/news/astros-cheating-scandal-explained/1ptq9e01ed4sr1ozgmjsznsd7h

Rosenthal, K. Drellich, E. (2019, November 12). *The Astros Stole Signs Electronically in 2017:* Part of a Much Broader Issue for Major League Baseball. https://theathletic.com/1363451/2019/11/12/the-astros-stole-signs-electronically-in-2017-part-of-a-much-broader-issue-for-major-league-baseball/

Young, R. (2021, October 18). *Pete Rose, Banned From Baseball for Betting on Games, Launches Gambling Podcast.* https://sports.yahoo.com/pete-rose-banned-from-mlb-baseball-for-betting-on-games-launches-gambling-podcast-231709480.html

Reed, W. (2021, June 19). *The Pete Rose Betting Scandal and Why He Should Be in the Hall of Fame. https://www.baseballspotlight.com/why-pete-rose-should-be-in-the-hall-of-fame/*

Neff, C. (1989, April 3). *Roses Grim Vigil. As Gambling Charges and the Media Engulfed Him, Pete Rose Awaited His Fate.* https://vault.si.com/vault/1989/04/03/roses-grim-vigil-as-gambling-charges-and-the-media-engulfed-him-pete-rose-awaited-his-fate

Verducci, T. (2004, January 12). *Pete Rose*: I Bet on Baseball. https://vault.si.com/vault/2004/01/12/pete-rose-quoti-bet-on-baseballquot

Beansprout, B. (Unknown). *The History of The Baseball Bat.* https://www.streetdirectory.com/travel_guide/40438/recreation_and_sports/the_histo

ry_of_the_baseball_bat.html#:~:text=William%20Shroyer%20patented%20the%20first,first%20little%20league%20aluminum%20bat.

Roberts, J. (2020, April 14). *The Great Cleveland Indians Heist of 1994.*

Means, J. (Unknown). *Why is Cork Banned in Baseball?*

Lengel, D. (2014, April 24). *Tar for the Course:* Yankees Pitcher Michael Pineda Busted for Using Foreign Substance.

Borcas, M. (2014, April 24). *Captain Obvious:* Michael Pineda, Pine Tar, and the Neck Smear That Shattered Baseball's Code of Silence.

Tool, T.C. (2021, March 27). *Here's the History of Basketball:* From Peach Baskets in Springfield to Global Phenomenon.

Klein, C. (2016, December 15). *Who Invented Basketball?* A Canadian is to Thank for One of America's Favorite Pastimes.

McCarthy, A. (Unknown). *How the Boston College Basketball Team Ended Jimmy Burke's Reign With Lucchese Crime Family.*

Perdum, D. (2014, October 3). *The Worst Fix Ever.*

Slotnik, DE. (2015, December 11). *John Williams, Versatile N.B.A, Player Known as Hot Rod, Dies as 53.*

Eden, S. (2020, January 20). *How Former Ref Tim Donaghy Conspired to Fix NBA Games.*

Butler, S. (2022, November 3). *What is a Burner Phone (and When to USe One)?*

Blitz, M. (2015, MArch 23). *The Infamous 1951 CCNY Points Shaving Scandal.*

Madden, B. (1995, February 13). *Nat Holmam's Record vs. Kentucky.*

Scott, H. (2012, December 6). *The 10 Most Controversial Players in College Basketball History.*

Rice, R. (1955, February 25). *The Bewildered Fixer.*

Tomlinson, S. (2013, October 14). Man That Led Shameful Basketball Team Who Pretended to be Disabled to Win Paralympic Gold Found Guilty of Fraud.

Kidwell, J. (2008, November 15). *226 Countries Can't Be Wrong.*

Unknown. (2022, September 12). *How and When Was Soccer Invented.*

Bonetti, M. (2014, May 17). *The Amazing Story of Italy's 1982 World Cup Hero Paolo Rossi.*

Nussbaum, B. Doherty, JE. (2021, February 22) *Italy's Guardia di Finanza:* Policing Financial Crime and Domestic Security in a Changing World.

Lehec, J. (2022, September 17). *The Calciopoli Scandal*: Juventus. .

Sergi, A. (2019, June 24). *How Mafia and Corruption Scandals Rocked Italian Football, Leaving Fans With a Crisis of Faith.*

Brischetto, P. (2022, December 18). *Diego Maradona Hand of God goal:* The story of a legendary World Cup moment.

Unknown. (2016, February 4). *Meet the 'Ndrangheta.*

Jones, T. (2016, December 1). *Inside Italy's Ultras:* The Dangerous Fans Who Control the Game.

Unknown. (2018, October 31). *Vincenzo Iaquinta:* Ex-Juventus Star Jailed in Mafia Case.

Cripps, S. (2014, May 6). *The Monster's Grandson:* Giuseppe Sculli and the 'Ndrangheta.

Majumdar, R. (2019, April 11). *The History of German Football.*

Falk, A. (2018, April 20). *How the Biggest Match Fixing Scandal in Beundesliga History Changed the German Game Forever.*

Unknown. (Unknown). *Arminia Bielefeld Statistics.*

Unknown. (2021, March 11). *German Legend Backs Bayern Ace to Break Long-Standing Records.*

Harding, L. (2005, November 18). *Two Years in Jail for Match-Fixing German Referee.*

Bairner, R. (2018, May 16). *France's Bribery Scandal:* The Story of Marseille's Tainted Champions Legue Trophy.

Sengupta, K. (1999, August 18). *Gambling Syndicate in Plot to Sabotage Soccer.*

Steele, J. (1999, August 21). *Gamblers Guilty of Match-rigging Scheme Face Jail.*

Nicholson, P. (2020, March 31). *Ukraine 'Ghost' Games Fool Bookies and Punters as Criminals Pull off Perfect Crime.*

Stone, S. (2015, March 2). *Ghost Games Betting Scam Costs Bookie Thousands of Pounds.*

Wahl, M. (2016, Unknown). *Diego Maradona:* Biography.

Malvany, K. (2022, April 2). *The Improbable Falklands War Still Resonates Decades Later.*

Platt, O. (2022, June 22). *Diego Maradona and the Hand of God:* The Most Infamous Goal in World Cup History.

John, E. (2009, November 15). *Frozen in Time:* The Aluminium Bat Affair, 14 December 1979.

Siddharth, V, (2020, February 13). *On this Day* - Michael Holding Kicks the Stumps, Mighty West Indies Stunned by New Zealand.

Adhikari, S. (2022, February 1). *41 Years Ago, The First Underarm Ball in International Cricket Was Bowled.*

Watson, G. (2013, January 16). *Bodyline:* 80 Years of Cricket's Greatest Controversy.

Varoutsos. E. (2022, October 20). *The Most Popular Sports in the World.*

Bujoy. (2022, February 1). *IPL History:* Most Expensive Player is Each IPL Season.

Roy, A. (2021, April 22). *Five Controversies that Rocked the IPL.*

Bhagchandani, U. (2022, July 22). *Who is Lalit Modi.*

Rowney, J. (2009, July 13). *The line between gamesmanship and cheating.*

Wion Web Team. (2022, June 5). *Harbhajan Singh Recalls Infamous Sreesanth Slapgate Row:* "I Made a Mistake, It Should not Have Happened.

Cricketnext Staff. (2014, February 10). *IPL Spot-Fixing Scandal:* How it Unfolded.

Manjunath, A. (2020, May 4). 5 match fixing scandals that shocked the world.

Usmani, M. (unknown). *Public Interest Litigation:* Its Origin and Meaning.

Laghate, G. (2013, May 24). *Spot-Fixing Impact:* IPL Viewership Drops 14%.

Cricketnext staff. (2021, August 28). *On This Day in 2010:* Spot-fixing Scandal That Rocked the Cricketing World.

Beasley, A. (2021, June 1). *The Hansie Cronje Match Fixing Scandal:* The Complete Story.

Banerjee, N. (2021, January 15). *Impressive Mohammad Azharuddeen Dreams of Playing 2023 World Cup for India.*

Webdesk. (2022, January 27). *Air Crash Consumes Hansie Cronje.*

Wilson, A. (2012, February 17). *Danish Kaneria Talked Mervyn Westfield Into Spot-Fixing, Court Told.*

Newman, P. (2020, March 18). *Bob Woolmer's Death:* An Event Almost Beyond Comprehension.

Zwar, A. (2021, December 10). *Bigger Than I'd Ever Imagined:* The 1981 Underarm Bowl That Lives on in Cricket Infamy.

Wertheim, J. (2021, August 6). *The Year the NFL Banned Two of its Biggest Stars for Gambling.*

Goodbread, C. (2020, November 13). *Paul Hornung, Packers Great and Hall of Famer, Passes Away at 84.*

Carter, B. (unknown). *Rozelle Made NFL What it is Today.*

Cripps, S. (2014, May 6). T*he mobster's grandson: Giuseppe Sculli and the 'Ndrangheta*. These Football Times.

Wharton, D. (2022, March 14). *Was it Hypocritical for the NFL to Suspend Calvin for Gambling?* Maybe Not.

Strackbein, N. (2022, August 2). *Steelers Brian Flores Responds to Dolphins Punishment for Tanking.*

Miller, B. (2022, unknown). *Breaking News: Bruce Beal Now Likely Out as Future Miami Dolphins Owner.*

ESPN.com news services. (2014, September 12). *Adrian Peterson booked, released.*

NFL.com (2022, August 2). *NFL announces findings and discipline following independent investigation of integrity of the game policy violations by the Miami Dolphins.*

Editors, History.com. (2007, September 9). *NFL Nabs New England Patriots in "Spygate" Scandal.*

Morin, R. (2022, January 29). *Remembering Deflategate*: What Really Happened? Did Tom Brady Cheat with New England Patriots?

NFL World. (2022, July w). *How Many Footballs Are Used in a Game?*

Wilcockson, J. (2003, April 2). *What Sort of Pirate?*

Fotheringham, W. (2004, February 27). *How the Pirate Hit the Rocks.*

Associated Press. (2013, July 24). *Probe Reveals Doping by Panatin, Ulrich in 1998.*

Martin, L. (2022, November 30). *What is a Normal Hematocrit Level?*

Associated Press. (2015, November 19). *Dr Michele Ferrari Ordered to Stand Trial in Biathlon Doping Investigation.*

McKay, F. (2011, February 16). *Tough on Doping, Tough on the Causes of Doping - Francesco Conconi and the Introduction of the H-Test.*

Kelso, P. (2004, February 19). *Pantanis Revelation of Torment.*

Fabrizi, M., & Ford, R. (2014). Sports Stories and Critical Media Literacy. English Journal, 104(1), 42.

Newswires. (2013, June 6). *Former Tour de France Winner Ullrich Admits to Doping.*

Homewood, B. (2012, August 25). *Jan Ullrich Proud of Tour de France Second Places.*

NBC. (2020, May 29). *Lance Armstrong, Jan Ullrich, and a Tour de France Rivalry that Brought Tears.* .

Reuters. (2006, May 26). *Ullrich Pulls out of Giro.*

Unknown. (2009, November 16). *Lance Armstrong Wins Seventh Tour de France.*

Seaton, M. (2012, October 10). *Lance Armstrong Team Ran Most Sophisticated Scheme in Sport.*

Deutschmann, J. (2022, February 15). *The Untold Truth of the First Tour De France Winner Maurice Garin.*

CBC sports. (2004, February 18). *Italy mourns cyclist Pantani*

Reuters. (2012, October 22). *Factbox:* Sponsors Drop Lance Armstrong.

News18, Sportsdesk. (2022, September 18). *Lance Armstrong Turns 51:* Where is the Former American Cyclist Now?

Dator, J. (2017, August 1). *The 7 Most Creative Cheating Stories in Cycling History.*

Redford, P. (2017, July 30). *53-Year-Old Italian Cyclist Caught Using Illegal Motor In Bike, Doesn't Even Win Race.*

Kevin, K. (2007, June 18). *Book Review:* Floyd Landis' Positively False.

Fox, S. (unknown). *A Brief History of the Tour de France.*

Martin, L. (2018, May 25). *Cycling Fans Taunt Chris Froome Over Failed Drugs Test with Giant Inhaler as He Goes on Solo Break at Giro d'Italia.*

Unknown. (2020, December 21). *How Much Does a MotoGP Cost?* .

Motorsport Magazine. (2021, May 1). *How Much Does an F1 Car Cost?*

Unknown. (2007, July 25). *'Stepney-gate' Scandal Rolls On.*

PistonHeads. (2007, July 4). *Nigel Stepney Under Investigation:* Bringing the Sport Into Disrepute.

Benson, A. (2014, May 2). *Nigel Stepney:* Ferrari "Spy-gate" Mechanic Dies in Road Accident.

Boxall-Legge, J. (2021, June 10). *The Biggest of F1 Cheating:* Spygate, Crashgate, and More.

Thorn, D. (2020, April 24). *The Forgotten Story of the 2005 San Marino Grand Prix.*

Wilde, J. (2022, September 25). *Flavio Briatore Discusses His New Role After Return to Formula* 1.

Somerfield, M. (2020, May 12). *Banned:* When F1 Teams Cheated the Minimum Weight Rules.

Crosse, J. (2021, June 3). *Why the DFV is the Greatest Racing Engine of All Time.*

Wilkerson, I. (2022, September 4). *5 Greatest NASCAR Legends.*

Samaddar, U. (2021, April 6). *These Are Some of the Biggest Cheaters NASCAR Has Ever Seen.*

Crisara, M. (2022, July 8). *Smokey Yunick Was NASCAR's Greatest "Cheater."*

Piscopo, N. (2018, September 28). *20 Race Car Drivers Who Cheated and Won (Only Some Got Caught).*

Gelston, D. (2022, July 25). *JGR Accepts Penalties Given to Hamlin, Busch, Apologizes.*

Turner, J. (2014, September 12). *Hamlin Crew Chief Says He Didn't Cheat.*

Zeller, B. (1993, July 1). *Schrader Suspended for Rules Violation\Driver, Owner to Miss Four Races.*

Hamilton, M. (2008, February 22). *The Joy of Six:* Motorsports Dirtiest Tricks.

Bowes, A. (2020, July 2). *The True Story of Richard Petty's NASCAR Dominance.*

Jenen, T. (2020, October 5). *Petty Blues* - An Illegal Car Sparked Controversy.

Kayer, J. (2009, July 13). *Mark Martin:* The Legend That May Never Be Remembered.

LA Times Staff. (2002, November 5). *Martin is Docked Points by Nascar.* .

Fraser, L. (2009, June 3). *Long's Life Sentence:* How Nascar Ruined Someone's Life.

News Source. (2021, June 18). *28 June 1997:* The Infamous Bite Fight Between Holyfield and Tyson.

Griffiths, D. (2014, January 6). *Who is Evander Holyfield?*

Editor, The Guardian. (2017, June 29). *Tyson, Holyfield Meet 20 Years After Ear Bite Fight in Las Vegas.*

Schwartz, J. (2022, April 22). *Mike Tyson's Worst-Ever Moments and Scandals Besides Airplane Attack.*

Ancestry.com®. (n.d.). *Margarito family history*. Margarito Name Meaning & Margarito Family History.

Guardian News and Media. (2009, February 11). *Boxing:* Antonio Margarito has been banned for one year over a substance found in his gloves.

Smith, T. (2019, January 11). *Antonio Margarito dishonored the sport by using illegal handwraps and should be banned from boxing.*

Writer, C. (2022, December 30). *Shane Mosley:* Record and stats. MartialBot.

Thompson, T. O'Keeffe, M. (2019, January 11). *Shane Mosley drops $12m defamation suit against BALCO founder Victor Conte, ending long legal battle.*

Publisher, M. (2018, March 07). *"Sugar's" unheard truth-* steroid scandal revealed.

Roth, M. (2017, September 18). *Dana White:* Victor Conte is a "two-faced" Piece of crap.

Thompson, T. Vinton, N. (2008, December 4). *"Sugar" Shane Mosley told grand jury of EPO use.*

Simonetti, AZ. (2016, December 29). *The nightmare of what Luis Resto did to Billy Collins has stayed with everyone it has touched.*

News, Boxing. (2020, April 7). *Judging the Sanctioning Bodies:* The IBF.

Gold, J. (2000, August 17). *IBF Founder Acquitted of Bribery. .*

Way, DL. (2022, December 12, updated). *Donovan Bailey:* Jamaican Born Canadian Sprinter.

Andre de Grasse (2022) *Team Canada* - Official Olympic Team Website.

Morgan, M. (2016, October 25). *Canadian sprinting legend Bailey calls on IAAF to "press reset" on records tainted by doping.*

Mackay, D. (2004, July 29). *The Kansas Cannonball is back in town and firing from the lip.*

Mackay, D. (2003, April 18). The dirtiest race in history 100m final, 1988.

Lynch, M. (2011, August 20). *Phil Mickelson and 10 Modern Golfers Who Under-achieved.*

Polychronis, J. (2022, June 8). *'Reckless': Mickelson opens up about "embarrassing" gambling losses amid $277m payday.*

Goldman, C. (2018, August 18). *Golf:* The Longest Records in PGA History.

Fish, M. (2020, April 30). *Noted gambler Billy Walters cleared to complete prison sentence at home.*

Sens, J. (2016, January 20). *A Look Inside Cheatings Role in Golf History.*

Nichols, BA. (2022, March 28). *Q&A:* Jane Blalock, Chevron's first champion on how Dinah Shore event transformed the LPGA as well as her bank account and what's keeping her out of the Hall of Fame.

Haigh, P. (2018, December 1). *Which snooker matches Yu Delu and Cao Yupeng fixed as both are banned over betting scandal.*

Associated Press (2018, December 1). *Chinese Snooker Players Yu Delu and Cao Yupeng Banned for Match-Fixing.*

Nunns, H. (2022, October 12). *Stephen Lee leaves door ajar for snooker comeback after 12-year match-fixing ban.*

PA Team. (2014, June 2022). *John Higgins Fortunate to Still Be Playing Snooker.*

Associated Press. (n.d.). *Gambling Bust Involves Tochet, Gretzky's Wife.*

Buccigross, J. (2006, February 14). *"Operation Slapshot" soap opera will blow over.*

Mooney, H. (2014, March 13). *Danish hockey players suspended, fired from team after game fixing scandal.*

Pak, E. (2021, December 3). *Tonya Harding and Nancy Kerrigan:* A Complete Timeline of Kerrigan's Attack and Aftermath.

Swift, EM. (2002, February 25). *Thorny Issue Canadian Pair David Pelletier and Jamie Sale Got Belated Gold Even as a Judging Scandal So Shook the Sport That it Brought Talk of Long Overdue Reform.*

Kasprak, A. (2002, February 11). *Is "Abortion Doping" a Real Practice?*

AP News. (1991, March 15). *Jockey Convicted of Hiding in the Fog.*

Farber, M. (2020, July 21). *The Curious Case of the Electrified Epee.*

Henson, M. (2016, August 11). *Sex and Gender in Hitler's Shadow: Dora Ratjen and the 1936 Olympics.*

Rugby Pass. (n.d.). *Details of All Blacks' 1995 World Cup poisoning revealed.*

Smythe, J. (2017, June 23). *Why are the All-Blacks so good?*

Aylwin, M. (2014, December 5). *Bloodgate on minds as Harlequins welcome back Leinster for first time.*

Devzone (n.d.). *Top quotes on practicing sportsmanship.*

About the Author

David Carlton is a child of 1970's and 80's Britain. An avid sports fan, with a keen interest in not only the history, but the weird, wonderful and more unscrupulous stories from across the world that only sport provides!

David is married, with three children and lives in Bedfordshire, England.

Also by David Carlton

A History of Irish Organized Crime

Printed in Great Britain
by Amazon

23863622R00089